Seasons
by the
Sea

For Harah

PAULA GREEN

Seasons by the Sea

A Coastal Garden in Australia

Photography Terry Hoey

BLOOMINGS
BOOKS

First published in Australia in 2001 by
Bloomings Books

Melbourne, Australia
Phone +61 3 9819 6363
Facsimile +61 3 9818 1862
sales@bloomings.com.au

Bloomings Books is a specialist publisher and distributor of horticultural
and natural history books.

The publisher would welcome readers' comments:–
warwick@bloomings.com.au

Designer: Jo Waite
Cover design: Terry Hoey and Jo Waite
Editor: Bryony Cosgrove
Photography: Terry Hoey
Publisher: Warwick Forge

National Library of Australia, Cataloguing-in-publication entry
    Green, Paula, 1951-.
    Seasons by the sea : a coastal garden in Australia.
    ISBN 1 876473 29 0.

    1. Green, Paula, 1951- – Homes and haunts – Victoria –
    Gippsland. 2. Seaside gardening – Victoria – Gippsland.
    3. Gardens – Victoria – Gippsland. I. Hoey, Terry.
    II. Title.

    635.099456

CONTENTS

FOREWORD

Gardens are inexhaustibly fascinating. That is, if they are true gardens, and not just a patch of slightly improved desolation sprawling around a house. In any true form, the garden is an exact cooperation of nature and culture. It bespeaks us, visually announcing that we are at home in the world: it is wilderness with clothes on. And it will soothe us all.

But cultivation does not just grow up like Topsy, particularly in a challenging environment. Paula Green's richly rewarding book not only tells us but shows us how a garden was created in harsh littoral bushland: sandy, demanding, visited by Bass Strait winds and in summer by dry northerlies. The Venus Bay she depicts is not some lush site of Aphrodite, but a coastal scrubland of muted tones, 'salt-laden winds and sand abrasion'.

Paula Green's prose is as lush, various and productive as the process she has charted here.

Her short sentences press upon one another, charged with colours, tastes and sounds. And she calls up processes: wrens darting, dahlias opening, vine leaves grovelling, the insidious creeping of couch grass, the construction of a stone wall, or the mulcher's pitchfork piling 'pyramids of shredded waste' onto endangered summer garden beds. She observes the hues and textures of everything, making the reader feel them, at the nerves' end.

What we can never forget in *Seasons by the Sea* is the natural, feral world throbbing just outside this garden, this orchard. And yet, nestling within that environment we have a little world like Andrew Marvell's:

What wondrous life is this I lead!
Ripe apples drop about my head;
The luscious clusters of the vine
Upon my mouth do crush their wine;
The nectarine, and curious peach
Into my hands themselves do reach.

Yes, the vibrant, sappy forces of nature can be coaxed into human friendship, but not without constant labour, and here is a book that tells us how.

If prose was ever like painting, Paula Green's is. She is as enquiring as John Wolseley, as harmonious as Renoir, as enchanted by tones and colours as Clarice Beckett. And this is done in the seemingly abstract medium of prose. Who else, since Gerard Manley Hopkins, could have written, 'Self-sown bronze fennel's feather dusters soften the straitlaced rose stems'? Or, turning indoors, 'The downy leaves and curly tendrils set off the frilly flowers', which uses three of what Keats's critics called Cockney adjectives, in a dancing, evocative row.

This is a book of food and foliage, foxes and finches. Green gives the reader a sense of human labour, but also of its rich produce; there are even recipes planted here and there. Turn to any page and you are going to marvel at its kinds of richness. And for all its cornucopia, you will never forget that this garden is lodged in the distinctive South Gippsland littoral.

Chris Wallace-Crabbe

DEDICATION

Terry and I are opposites. We are a hare-and-tortoise team. I race around. Weeds whiz through the air and mounds of mulch are whisked away in moments. But I am a flash-in-the-pan. Terry has the stamina of a Trojan and the skill of an artisan. He can turn his hand to anything. He's jack-of-all-trades: builder, brickie, carpenter, plumber, fencer and Mr Fixit-odd-jobs-get-Terry-onto-it handyman.

We have a good system. I dream up harebrained schemes and he goes along with them. I suggest 'What about this?' and 'How about that?' He agrees, then asks, 'Where's my list?' If he does mind, he's not letting on.

INTRODUCTION

The seasons broke me in as a gardener. Summer sun pulled me out of the dark and dried my 'wet-behind-the-earsness'. Autumn gales pruned my misconceptions and cut out the dead wood. Winter hit me with the cold truth. Winds whacked me around the face until I made some sense of it all. I was all thumbs till spring turned my fingers green and I got a grip on the big picture. Showers watered hopes. Thoughts took root. Plans poked through. Possibilities sprang to life. Ideas grew.

The seasons spun like a revolving dance floor. When I first jumped on I had two left feet and fell flat on my face. As the seasons circled the tunes became familiar, and I picked up the beat. I practised my steps: two forward, one back. The seasons lead and I follow. I still stumble. My footwork's nothing fancy. But in the garden I dance to the rhythm of the seasons. Round and round and round we go.

BUSH AND BEACH

In 1980 Terry and I bought seven hectares of remote coastal bushland at Point Smythe, Venus Bay, adjoining the Cape Liptrap Reserve, South Gippsland. It was just a stone's throw from Anderson's Inlet. A track snaked through tea-tree forest to a ready-made clearing. We thought it would be easy. Bush. Beach. Build a house. Make a garden. But we were way off the mark. We were babes in the woods and unprepared for the hard slog ahead.

At first we were housebound, tied up by learn-the-ropes building and the stay-at-home jobs of caring for our newborn son and daughter. Skirting the boundaries, gathering firewood and baskets of banksia cones, we didn't venture further than the beach. The forest seemed unfamiliar and mysterious. We felt vulnerable blundering through a neck of no-man's-land that stuck out into the ocean; intruders in an ancient landscape.

We had to find our place here. We explored the mudflats along Anderson's Inlet, the tracks that trailed the tea-tree maze to the Venus Bay surf beach and to the tip of Point Smythe.

During these walks we began to get our bearings, slowly unveiling some of the secrets, colours, textures, sounds and smells of these wild gardens.

Anderson's Inlet

We weave our way through banksias, backing the salt marsh. Fluoro-green coastal wattle tips stroke our cheeks. Beard heath perfume tickles our noses. Waves of silver eyes squeak through low-lying branches. A fringe of scruffy-headed paperbarks stands ankle-deep in the tidal waters. When king tides flood the marsh the trees wade up to their knees.

Townsend's Bluff sticks out its acned nose. Black swans poke the mudflats. Ibis graze the tidal pasture. Cormorants fish. The half-tide curves a crusty salt line. Sand worms scribble in the wet sand. Pearl-pink pipi shells lie face down. The crumpled waters reflect slate-grey cloud shadows skipping across the landscape. The sound of water slapping is pitched higher than the base notes booming on the back beach.

Knobby club rush brush-strokes a silver sea of grass. Twinkled through these peaty gardens is creeping brookweed, its lustre like fallen stars. Rust-tipped beaded glasswort meadows hug the airless earth. Dragonflies glide over lagoons. Bleached-blonde tussocks wave wigs in the wind. Low afternoon sun spins their straw into gold. Manna gums stand head and shoulders above saltbush scrambling across the track. Kangaroos paw-print the pipi-shell-flecked sand. Roos graze silver spinifex blades that stab right into the mangroves.

White mangroves mark the seaward boundary. Squat stands streamered with seagrass and draped with seaweed are among the most southern in the world. The wax-leaved trees hold their heads above the choking mudflats and drowning waters. Waves lick their rubbery roots, pneumatophores that resemble tangled snorkels for aerial breathing. Green mangrove crabs tiptoe around rotted root stumps.

Our bare feet squelch through the mudflats. Armies of soldier crabs retreat and advance with the tide. The crabs scuttle forwards rather than sideways, crumpet the sand then corkscrew into burrows. Sandflies sting our shins. Propped on eskies, fishermen throw in a line. Two women churn the sludge for sandworms to hook a flathead or mullet on the tide turn. Plastic buckets stink of bait and fish heads. Seagulls float up, up and away. A fisherman wades shin deep scraping scales, slitting and gutting his catch. Pacific gulls squabble over the scraps. The birds squawk, niggle and bicker as the victor snatches the spoil in his scarlet-tipped beak and soars skyward.

We wander the marsh, foraging through chaffy saw-sedge, snatching at salt-bitten stems and fleshy leaves of beach-grown bower spinach, sea celery and juice-sweet heath berries.

Venus Bay

We tread the bush track to go walkabout to the surf beach. Even in blistering heat the tea-tree tunnel is shaded, sheltered and grotto-cool. Moss-furred pathways cushion our bare feet. Sea mumblings and creaking branches are the only sounds. Otherwise invisible, spiders' webs are lit by afternoon sun.

Butterflies escort us. Playing chasey, they brush wing tips, flap around our hair, fan our shoulders and flutter down like rusty autumn leaves. Spot lit, they flicker through spears of light, defying all attempts to be caught.

The tea-tree forest seems ancient. Dingy hollows and dips conceal wombat and echidna hidey-holes. Close to shore the trees appear as sailboats in dock, rocking in the wind and anchored in earth. Trunk masts creak like rigging as they strain and launch their spider-webbed sails towards the sea.

We scramble up into hunch-backed dunes. Salt spray tangs our tongues and dusts the light with milky crystals. High on the cliff top a westerly wind whacks our faces and electrifies our hair. To the north-west, the coast is cratered with Cape Paterson's cracked cliffs, sea-gouged caves and wave-worn rock platforms. To the south-east, Cape Liptrap's tanned arm muscles its way into Bass Strait.

Salt-laden winds and sand abrasion have dwarfed plants waist-high. Spindly drifts of coastal rosemary, silver daisy bush, cinnamon-stemmed correa, cushion bush, wattle and tea-tree mimic topiary.

A Pacific gull hang-glides, riding the thermals. Aluminium gulls row oar legs across the surf sky. Wind-winged, we float down the dune, screaming to be heard against the wave crash.

SEASONS

After I first met Terry, he went overseas on a year's study leave. He sent me a book from America, which he had crafted himself. It was hand-bound in blue-gold floral cloth. Hand-made parchment separated sheets of rice paper. Inside the cover a hidden compartment (containing a packet of gourd seeds) read 'Do not open until spring'.

His simple watercolour paintings showed a gourd's cycle from seed to fruit. It began with winter's bare earth, progressing to seeds sprouting in spring, to sprawling summer vines and to the autumn celebration of a harvest: a take-your-breath-away tapestry of fruits and flowers in golds and blues and rich earth tones. It was an omen of our future lives together.

The familiar passing of the seasons shapes patterns, rituals and chores. Death and decay, growth and fruition stir different changes and awakenings. The garden rearranges itself like clockwork.

Each season has its own joys and limitations. We re-sow, re-weed and re-reap but it's never a case of been-there-done-that or here-we-go-again. Each one holds new garden experiences to savour.

The seasons slot into succession. Spring follows on from winter, summer takes up where spring left off, autumn has its turn, hands the reins to winter and I change partners. But sometimes the seasons shuffle themselves around. The weather's put on hold: a trans-seasonal in-between time, suspended. Asleep but with one eye open. Nearly summer, not quite autumn, almost spring or post-winter. It's as if even nature needs a break. The sun hides its face behind clouds. The wind catches its breath. Rain can't be bothered. Buds won't open. Seeds refuse to come up. Birds don't sing a note. The music stops playing and we sit this one out.

Spring

Spring whispers through a winter limping on its last legs. It creeps up on me just when I'm not looking. It comes like the kiss of life. Cold days are blown away by spring's warm breath. It's been sleeping in my arms all winter. It uncurls in the sun, yawns, stretches and rubs the sleep from green eyes. Cheeks flush. Its fresh face sparkles. Its heart rate quickens. Spring twitches with birth pangs. Wide awake, it takes my hand. Spring is stepping out in a new dress.

Waders migrating from Siberia, Alaska and Asia streak the skies along Anderson's Inlet. Greenshanks, sharp-tailed and curlew sandpipers and red-necked stints navigate by sun and stars, coastlines and mountain ranges. Thousands of birds journey to the warmer weather and plentiful food supply along the mudflats and salt marsh, where the Tarwin River enters Bass Strait via Anderson's Inlet. The seabirds' presence marks our seasons as their time here matches the garden's peak periods.

Winter's drapes are drawn open. Tea-tree bursts into bloom. Scrubby scalps shake heads full of dandruff. The landscape seems snow-capped. Cream paperbark blossoms are daubed along the salt marsh. Purple noon-flowers and yellow water-buttons crawl among the dunes. Guinea flowers' buttery cups light up the roadsides. In tea-tree shade, hard-to-see fairies' orchids sparkle like pink stars.

Days are longer. Thornbills fuss with beakfuls of bark to thatch hooded nests. Bronze-wings' chestnut heads and shoulders gleam in the sun. The pigeons nod about, gathering twigs for flimsy nests then fly off with a clatter of wings. Willie wagtails dart about in jerky flight, snatching insects.

Wrens tag along as my sidekicks. The males glitter in spiffy turquoise and black jackets. They are devoted fathers, fetching titbits to stuff in the beaks of the young bobbing behind them. Harems of fawn jenny-wrens bounce about on dainty stilt legs. Males supposedly mate for life but come courting, offering beaks full of flowers, playing the field at other females' nests.

When the kitchen doors slide open, the wrens flit about the floor, squeaking like feathered mice or little wind-up toys. They join me for brunch on the verandah, nibbling crumbled fetta at my feet, skipping and jittering around my toes. In the garden, families whiz down in waves, scattering to feed in circles, wagging aerial-like tails as they ricochet across hedges. Wrens don't venture far from shrub protection; they get a bit twitchy out in the open. When startled, they fly off in a flurry of wing beats.

I daydream along the surf beach. Nature is spring-cleaning. Soap-flake tea-tree blossoms smell lemon fresh. The sun is a copper-pot boiling. The sea is streaky with blue beads of bleach. Wind spin dries and scuffs sand squeaky clean. Rubber-glove sponges scour shell crockery. The ocean lathers soapsuds. Its spray-mist steam curls collars and irons them flat. Pegged across a string of cloud, seagulls flap like laundry whiter-than-white. The wringer-wind rub-a-dub-dubs along the rippled washboard sand. It is a carpet beater bashing the shadow-woven scrub airing on the dunes.

The dark lifts off the dawn. A butcherbird alarm rings. Crickets tick tock. A wattlebird announces the news. A thornbill whistles. The wind shuffles as if in slippers. Kookaburras toss their heads back and gargle. The crumpet sun pops up. The morning is washed with light. Rosellas prattle on talkback. Radio birdsong is broadcast all day. Fairy wrens twitter and trill. Silver eyes warble. I eavesdrop on the private conversations of spinebills chatting 'tee tee tee' as they sip from correa cups.

After spending dopey days by winter fires, my callouses throb from digging. Muscles twinge. Even if the garden's closed, it's business-as-usual. Messy paths are scratched with a straw broom, bad-hair hedges are short-back-and-sides trimmed. But after being on its not-a-hair-out-of-place best behaviour, the garden lets go. So does the gardener. If she can be bothered, she goes through the motions of pulling waist-high weeds and dumping them on the heap. The go-slow work is relaxing without the glitz of show biz. Spring's a hard act to follow.

I dawdle along the well-tramped track clanking a bucket of roses. My next-door neighbour Neil is outside, curved in a deckchair. His white beard is tinged lemon as if dyed in wattle blossoms. His eyes seem like slits of sky. Neil's natural garden is stunning. Club rush spiked with cinnamon baubles contrast with yellow groundsel daisies. I give a 'Yoo-hoo'. He uncoils, waves his 'Never-better-can't-complain' wave and lowers the billy onto ash. His weather-beaten hands are as wrinkled as banksia bark. His eyes water when he spots the roses. He greets each one as a long-time-no-see friend on a first-name basis. Over mugs of tea he spins yarns woven through his long lifetime as a gardener. Though I have heard the stories before, versions vary and I am all-ears until the billy and tears of laughter run dry.

A wide-as-an-arm-span manna gum local kids call the honey tree scrambles along the Inlet, a couple of kilometres away. I plan to strip off a few seed heads, stuff a paper bag in my back pocket and wobble off on my bike. Faint tea-tree scent still drifts through the wind-clipped dunes.

A cloud of smoke flickers pink galahs. A bushranger bails me up: a wallaby masked in bandit-black stripes. The wheels crunch the gravel road that winds down to the Inlet. I park the bike, scuff the salt-and-peppered peat-sand and head for the honey tree. The beach is scarred with fallen relics, victims of tidal flooding and erosion.

The tree lounges on its belly like a sleeping mermaid. Silver bark echoes fish scales sweating in the sun. Her wide rump sprawls right to the water. Toe roots strain to grip the soil. The tide tugs at her torso. Tangled limbs mimic splintered hands. Withered fingers taper down. Her nails tear the sand. Bark ribbons shawl her hunched shoulders and ivory arms. Eucalyptus perfumes her breath.

Some nights I have heard her moaning, her bones creaking and her thighs scraping sand. I have caught glimpses of the tide stroking her fingers and the sun towelling her dry. I have seen her rise from her haunches, toss back her garland hair and thrust forward to meet the sea.

The trunk is a cave wall gallery. Scribbles seem like messages in ancient code. The cracked skin crawls with ants. Toffee-sap drips. Summer blossoms will drown the tree in nectar. The Aborigines collected manna, the edible sugars that crystallise on the leaves. My boots shatter bark scrolls as I snap off pointed buds. Criss-cross cups spill seed dust into the bag.

We balance self-preservation with a treed environment and burn off well before summer. Twigs and bracken are raked into peaks. On drizzly overcast mornings, heaped-up bonfires smoulder and crackle. Smoke curls around the homestead.

The garden summons me to witness the morning's miracles.

Any flaws are forgiven. I sing its glories as if for the first time. All is right with the world. But spring turns its back on me, looks over its shoulder. Eyelids are heavy. The heartbeat's getting fainter. Short of breath, spring closes its hands, then slips away. Faint footsteps pad closer. Summer's hot on our heels. Hefty temperatures give spring the boot.

Summer

Summer enters without knocking. Flexes its muscles, elbows its way in and sends spring packing. The season is a celebration of our own private Garden Fest. Bush Mardi Gras. We kick off our work boots and kick up our heels. We knock off early, roll up late or chuck it in all together. Seedlings sunbake and soak up a few rays. Vegetables swell. Fruits ripen. Seed heads snap, crackle and pop open.

The sky is jet-lined with streamers. Fairy-floss clouds sky-write 'Welcome'. Wrens blow a stop-work whistle. The ocean beats a drum roll. A lilium quartet trumpets 'Summer Time and the Livin' is Easy'. Nasturtiums blare on cornet. Butternuts play trombone. In frilly skirts gladdies are a go-go. Dahlias nod their heads in time. Crickets shake maracas. Bees hum along on paper and comb.

Rosellas are wandering minstrels. Roses dab on perfume, scatter scent and shower petals on paths. Late poppies wave coloured flags. A vine wears a passionflower behind its ear. Fruit trees are strung with candy. Sunlight licks toffee apples. Butterflies pattern heliotrope with paper lanterns. Weeds gatecrash the party. Sunflowers smile. Kookaburras are hysterical. A crowd of calendulas don sunbonnets. Beetles dress in harlequin costume. Frogs make announcements over the PA system. A chook cheers. On the washing line, trousers walk on air. Buttoned sleeves wave 'Hello'. Growing pace speeds up.

Living pace slows down. We siesta in the hammock to the tinkle of ice-cubes and the smell of melon rind.

On listless afternoons we spread out rugs, quilts and cushions. Dead grass is scattered with leaves, seed cones and kangaroo dung. We sprawl beneath borage-blue skies, the shade of straw hats and big bent banksias. We snooze to the drone of blowies, then wake, blurry-eyed and groggy, limbs prickling with pins and needles. Snarling jet-skis, speedboats and kids cooeeing in the Reserve snap us back to the real world.

Under a beach-ball sun and zinc-cream clouds, sandcastle dunes are decorated with people. Wave crests froth like beer ice-cold. Bats crack cricket balls. Kids call 'LBW'. Dads doze. Lines are cast. Reels hiss and sinkers spin on bendy rods. Toddlers squeal, spilling sea water from plastic buckets. Hot flesh sizzles in coconut oil and the smell of sunscreen. Noses peel. Shuttlecock gulls soar through the air.

Sweet bursaria smells honey-warm. Cottonwool flowers are dabbed all over the crown. Wartime scientists discovered that the leaves soaked in water release an inky blue pigment that works as a natural sunscreen. We blot it on sweaty faces and smear it over our arms.

On calm days at high tide we drag our beached 'tinny' down to the Inlet. I roll up my shorts, unravel the rope, hurl the anchor into the bow and yank the starter motor. The engine stutters. The boat bucks in the swell. Hand on tiller, we swerve off, dodging sandbars and keeping a close eye on channel markers. The engine drones at the stern and the boat thumps as waves whack the bow. Salt spray spatters our faces and stings our eyes as our coastline slips behind us.

She-oaks hang across the cliff tops. Stints and plovers prod the mud for crustaceans. Curlews inject beaks for ghost shrimps. Ibis dunk their bills, puncturing the mud skin. Little Mirror sailboats hurtle towards us, dipping into the choppy swell. The wind snaps spinnakers. Windsurfers whiz by. Hoop-sails crack. Although Inverloch is thirty kilometres by car, depending on tide and sandbars, we can zip across the Inlet in ten minutes.

The boat skims across the Tarwin River. Drowned mangrove forests resemble a bonsai landscape. Dairy cattle moan. Round hay bales roll across paddocks smelling of aftershave.

Pale-fleshed paperbarks lean along the shore. We skid on the greasy flat water, sliding by the tide line stained on reed stalks and stumps. The bow wave curls as the propeller beats the whitewater to froth.

Our journey is silent but for the engine drone, hissing grasses, garbled dialogue of golden plovers all talking at once, chittering grebes and the hacksaw screeching of pin-legged swamp hens wading through reeds, flicking tails and dipping scarlet bills into the sludge. We flash by cormorants and coots roosting in mangroves and egrets propped on scummy water markers. Ibis sickle weeds marinating in mud. Black swans bend their loopy necks. Hidden among the mudflats, swans' nests are heaped with dried grasses and reeds stuck with slime.

Pelicans sail by, hoisting baggy bills, pink silk spinnakers in the breeze. A swamp harrier's V-shape skirts the open country. The boat punts into the mud-stained shore. We cut the motor. The boat drifts. I drop anchor. We eel-slip into the shallows and wade shin-deep to shore.

Summer days peel off the calender like sun-blistered skin. We lose all track of time but the garden's body clock ticks over. Mother nature is bang on time, winding her pocket watch and sticking to her won't-wait schedule. But sometimes she sets her clock too fast. Lettuces are ready too early. We arrive too late. It's use-it or lose-it when tomatoes ripen too quickly and we can't keep up.

We get up early to beat the heat. Later in the day we swim to the sandbars dotted with ibis to lie in the shallows, but this morning we hike to the surf beach. In the open-air bathroom we soak in the ocean tub. The window sky is hung with fluffy towels of cirrus cloud. Sea sponges float. Back-scrubbing waves wash us up and down as we bob on the wave crests like rubber duckies. The undertow sucks our toes. Low tide pulls the plug. Feet print the sand as we straggle back, shivery and surf-charged. Our hair drips. Shirts cling to skin scratchy with salt, prickled with sun and tingling from wave foam.

In the mussel-purple night Terry flounders along the shallows. The dark hisses with mosquitoes. The ocean roars on the back beach. Satin swans shawl around him. An ibis barks. Broken sounds from Inverloch carry across to Maher's Landing. Thigh-high waders stir the soupy sand. His hand scythes the underwater, drags a torch wand in a swirling figure eight, curling seagrass around the lamp head. Fish flick around his shins. White knuckles hold a spear above the beam. He lunges, hurls the spear and by chance more than skill, skewers a snook into the murky sand. The fish thrashes, blood-smudging the water. Terry slips the body into the net bag dripping behind him.

In late summer heat-haze the atmosphere shimmers. The landscape's a smeared finger painting. Heat scratches at the tin roof. Birds are quiet. Ringtail possum tails, disguised as curled fern fronds, hang out of scrubby nests. Resident roos flop in the shade. Grubby-feathered chooks flap out dust baths under grapevines.

The ducks sleep with their heads tucked under their wings. We move in slow motion. Our pores are dust-clogged. Sandpaper skin is sticky with flies. Hot sand burns bare feet.

Banded tiger snakes writhe up trunks probing for nests. We become snake-conscious. All ears for twig-snap or rustle of leaf litter. All eyes for the flick of a lizard's tongue or a twitch of shadow. When coiled hose, shoelace or twig turn into snakes, we don't move a muscle.

Summer breathes down our necks. The bush broods hot under the collar. It's bonfire dry. A bronze-wing beeps a warning. Time-bomb crickets tick tick tick. Strips of paperbark are fuses waiting to be lit. Banksia cones resemble hand grenades. Leaves drop. We are always aware of the possibility of bushfire and mentally rehearse our survival plan.

Hands shade our eyes as we read the sky for messages. The weather reports no change. Later in the day, wind gives a warning. Storm cloud threatens. Tree tops tremble. Withered leaves scroll. Cornstalks rustle. Wattle pods snap, curl and split.

A sea breeze blows cool-as-cologne kisses. Bamboo blinds bump against hot windows. Rose-coloured light clears the haze. A plink on the roof eases tension. Drops fizz in the dust. The combination of hissing rain, bacteria in the soil and tea-tree-eucalyptus oil creates a tingling scent. Water trickles down the earth's throat. It spills down banksia trunks, gushes down spouting to the pond and pumps through leaf veins like green blood. Branches drip. Sand sinks. Water colours wash. Dyes run. Skin-and-bone plants flesh out. It's a good drop. Hard drinkers throw back drinks-on-the-house till after hours. Tomatoes have a few. Dahlias go on a bender.

Drenched in twilight we stumble through the tea-tree for a swim. Warm rain creeps across our skin streaky with dust. The muggy night is scratched with a golden plover's 'kree kree kree'. We peel off wet clothes. The tide licks our toe tips as we smell baked mud and passionfruit-perfumed mangrove flowers. We slip into the blood-warm water. Rain drops taste of creme de menthe. The miracle of the moon turns the water into wine.

In the dim light of dusk on this late summer evening our phantom shapes drift like garden ghosts-who-walk. We float as if figures from a Chagal painting or players in *A Midsummer Night's Dream*. White, night-scented tobacco perfumes my wrists. The click of crickets and gurgle of possums calling one another replaces fading birdsong. Our whispers trail off in the darkness.

Dusty moths flutter in the foliage. Bats flap in the tea-tree tops. The night is coloured deep-sea blue. A cloud-veiled moon lights up pale surfaces. White cosmos and roses shimmer with an eerie luminosity. The platinum bush turns to beaten silver. The semi-dark topiarises shrubs. Banksias seem like silhouettes. A masked barn owl floats through the chilled air. We hear the whoosh of its wings only after it passes. A distant, hoarse screech confirms it wasn't an illusion.

Autumn

Rain butts out the fag end of summer. Skies are smoke-free. Summer takes it last drag, runs short of breath and calls it quits. Autumn watches with amber eyes, half-open, half-closed. Rustles around at a slower pace. The cuckoo-shrike's mournful purring tells her melancholy mood.

The dawn orchestra shifts. The sound scape changes from wrens' trills, finches' peeps and silver eyes' squeaks to the butcherbird's piping song, magpies carolling and wattlebirds' cracked voices.

The sun shrivels. The light dwindles. The sea sighs. Another summer passes without the threat of tiger snakes sliding like ripple lines of heat, without the horror of bushfire, nagging blowies, the sting of march flies, slapping sandflies, blood-splattered legs and scratchy scabs around the ankles. The wind threshes grass heads, stripping, winnowing and harrowing. The garden is left to its own devices. Withered wands burst with seeds that sprout in the warm, wet dust. Grass-fuzz patches the lawn's receding hairline.

Gales blast leftover leaves from fruit trees. 'Mutton bird winds' carry fattened seabirds from the Bass Strait islands and Anderson's Inlet on their return journey to Northern Hemisphere breeding grounds. We sense the birds' departure as it signals the colder months ahead. Growth in the garden will decline until they come round again.

Rains lick leaves clean. Steady showers firm the dry sand. The smell of wet earth sweetens the air. After weeks of relentless heat there is a sense of quiet and clarity. Bracken fronds unfurl viridian green. The forest's form is shaped by dull-sheened trunks. Tea-tree tinkles with rain crystals. The bush sparkles with imitation jewellery: necklaces, bracelets and tiaras. Spiders' webs drip diamantes, marcasites and rhinestones.

We pick the last of the pumpkins before skies hurl hail. Balls of ice jackhammer the roof. Ice crusts the skylights. Transparent crystals slide down and melt in the sun showers.

Mist rolling in from the ocean seems like the earth's own breath. It sprinkles sugary kisses on my lips and tingles my tongue with sherbet. Silvers turn to pewter. Cloud clears. Sunlight dazzles. Rushes blaze gold. Bronzed banksias are tarnished amber. The landscape resembles a copperplate etching drying in the sun.

The bush doesn't rust with corroded colours of exotic autumn gardens. The native trees shed leaves all year though colour changes are subtle. Male she-oaks toss hennaed dreadlocks around in the wind. Winter re-dyes the tassels grey-green. Banksias and wattles carpet-weave the forest floor in clay and ochre. Bursaria's gloss-green and tan seed capsules stand out against dark trunks. Kangaroo apples' lemon and orange fruits match the courtyard's cumquats and lemons. The garden is splashed with berry-red rose hips, riesling-coloured grapevine leaves and the gold of shrivelled apples still dangling. Curled-up vine leaves slide along the verandah.

We harvest wild food. Banging billies and rustling plastic bags, the family tramps along the rain-washed road that trails east. Leather bracken ferns stroke trouser legs. Bidgee-widgees burr socks. Wind whistles through she-oaks beaded with raindrops. Clouds seem hand-painted. The ceramic sky is slip-glazed. Its chalky blue is paler than deeper blue summer skies. Our bones are still rattling from the early morning chill.

On private land in low valleys, blackberries spread like small-town gossip through environmentally conscious landowners are grubbing them out. We shortcut through a wire-strained fence. Canes have gone haywire. Green tentacles droop with ebony fruit. Thorny stems hook my jumper, snag my hair and prick my bleeding fingers fumbling through wet leaves.

The first ping in the bucket gives off a syrupy smell. The kids' teeth are gritty with seeds. Lips are smeared with port-wine bruises. Tongues are stained aubergine. We straggle back, scratches stinging. We cook up a tart devoured with whipped cream and tea, joking around the kitchen table, feeling close from the day's simple pleasures.

Blackberry Jam

Pile a couple of kilos of blackberries into a pan. Add one and a half to two kilos of sugar, depending on preferred sweetness. Throw in a few half-ripe sour berries. This is high in pectin and helps jam to set. Boil down until thick, stirring from time to time to prevent sticking. When cool, ladle into jars.

Blackberry tart holds pride of place in my battered scrap/cookbook. The book is packed with recipes pencilled on shopping dockets, paper bags, backs of envelopes and pages torn from exercise books. This light and flaky pastry, best made on a marble bench-top, is adapted from my mother's original recipe. She whipped it up on a Sunday after we kids trudged home swinging billies brimming with berries picked along country roads.

Blackberry Tart Flaky Pastry

250 grams cold butter
250 grams plain flour
pinch salt
50 mls cold water

Filling

blackberry jam

Grate butter over flour. Rub butter into flour with the palm pushing dough away from you until it comes together. Add salt and water. Don't overwork. Cover. Rest pastry in fridge for an hour. Roll out and press into a pie dish. Trim edges. Blind bake in moderate oven (180°C) for fifteen minutes until firm. Spread on generous layer of jam. Decorate with leftover pastry strips. Bake in very hot oven until pastry is crisp. Dust with icing sugar. Serve with cream.

Showers and sunny spells bring hidden harvests. Fungal threads swell overnight. Wild mushrooms, toadstools and wrinkled puffballs push their way through leaf mulch like buttons through buttonholes. Fungal flora has such beauty. Velvet caps teeter on inky parasols. Stems verandah raggy toadstools. Luminous oranges and reds, flecked white, glow against lime-green moss.

The sun-dappled forest seems enchanted. Caramel umbrellas mimic cafes for fairy folk. On nights near Easter, smudgy, glow-in-the-dark fungi lure us outside. The fungi radiate a moony light from within. In daylight, the white-fleshed, ruffled oyster mushrooms tiered around stumps seem so ordinary. After a week or so, they rot to slime.

Mushrooming is a family tradition. Damp earth smells of leaf mould as my knife slices through stems. The kids layer domed cups upside-down in the basket. Saucer-sized mushrooms resemble broad-brimmed hats. I flick my fingers across the pleated gills. Field mushrooms smell musty-sweet but it's the taste that's quintessential to the season. Over open-fire coals the pan sizzles with the earthy perfumes of garlic, onion and black flesh withering in a nob of melted butter. We splash in red wine, olive oil and balsamic vinegar. Sprinkled with roughly chopped parsley and served with pasta or gnocchi, the sauce and steaky flavours linger on the palate.

Terry makes this easy recipe for mushroom pie. The flaky pastry recipe for blackberry tart works equally well with this.

Mushroom Pie

flaky pastry
2 diced onions
1 or 2 cloves garlic
olive oil
250 grams mushrooms
1 cup chicken stock
few drops balsamic vinegar
handful chopped chives or parsley

Custard

200 mls cream
2 eggs
pinch salt
cracked black pepper

Fry onions and crushed garlic in olive oil until slightly caramelised. Throw in roughly chopped mushrooms. Sweat down for a couple of minutes. Pour in chicken stock and a shake of balsamic vinegar. Reduce until moisture is cooked out. Mix in herbs. Beat cream and eggs, salt and pepper. Combine all ingredients.

Line deep pie dish with rolled-out pastry. Pre-cook in oven at 160°C for 15-20 minutes.

Pour filling into pastry case and bake for another 25 minutes until pastry is crusty.

Candlewick banksia flowers flicker lemon-bronze against resin-stained trunks. Bottlebrush lie on the ground like sleeping baby echidnas cradled in fallen leaves. Younger toothed leaves are saw-blade sharp. Big-bodied banksias are moody but the trees transform in sunlight. When the sun strikes the sand, light shoots back into the sky, silvering the white under-leaves. Wind gusts turn the banksias inside out and the trees flash like a tinfoil forest. Punch-drunk on nectar, wattlebirds' dawn cackles wake any guests who expected a sleep-in. Twiggy nests propped in the forks of branches camouflage streaky plumage.

The whip-bird lives a secretive life. His nest is hidden in tea-tree. He's shy, fanning his tail and scratching around in leaf litter when he thinks no one's watching, yet his sharp whip-crack explodes through the bush. A couple of times I've caught glimpses of his courtship dance. He performs the pantomime deep in the theatre-dark forest. Dressed in an olive-green jacket, he ruffles his crested, black head-dress and hops about whistling and chuckling, quite chuffed with himself.

We often sight brown falcons seesawing in the sky and circling the dunes. Sometimes they perch on posts around the garden, ready to swoop off with a bush rat, a skink or a small bird. Screeching as she vanishes, the female's wide wingspan, blue-grey feathers and stiff legs are just visible against the scrub.

By chance, we spot stick insects climbing along branches. These pencil-thick sci-fi creatures are twiggy replicas of the sepia surrounds. Bleached-brown legs are matchstick-thin. Bulging goggle-eyes are their only giveaway.

Pygmy possums scamper round the kitchen at night. Males are larger, cheekier and squeakier than the females. They are about the size of a small mouse, though their tail is curlier, fur silkier and snout more pointed. I have unfolded them in the morning, snuggled up in a tea towel.

Possums show up for apple slices and muesli. Bunny-sized ringtails have rounded ginger ears, pointy, whiskered snouts and hazelnut eyes. White-tipped pipe-cleaner tails curl around a finger. We find them sleeping in a slipper on the verandah during the day. At night we hear them hissing along the roof and stripping the grapevines.

Towards the end of the season the days wilt, wash away in the rain and slip into the shadows. May winds snuff out autumn's flame and shout a warning for winter. Along the Inlet, nature celebrates autumn evenings with an impromptu outdoor cabaret. Ribbon clouds streamer the sky. The horizon line is strung with gold party lights, blinking, winking like fallen stars, masquerading as the lights of Inverloch.

Centre stage, the sky hangs a disco ball moon. It floodlights the waters sparkling silver lamé. Pairs of paper-boat figures glide by in the shadows. Dressed in dinner suits and black gowns, the silhouettes are spotlit as swans. Squeaky songs duplicate clarinets as crickets accompany on percussion, the distant surf booms base, entertaining us with their late-night magical music.

Winter

A shrike thrush rings in the changing season. This clear, one-note call differs from spring's song. The thrush's company is as welcome as the return of long-gone friends. Family groups are out and about skipping up trunks, poking bark and begging for cheese. Thrushes are charming, inquisitive birds that cock their heads as if to say, 'What's cookin'?' A pale-beaked female pecks crumbs from my palm and, like a singing telegram, flies off, announcing 'Winter'.

The crooning ocean calls. The back beach is deserted. A metal sky and galvanised sea blend into a flat-as-fibro horizon. We are at the end of the earth. Seabirds scream. Wind sculpts dunes and stings our faces with grains glass-sharp. Our eyes squint from salt spray. The sea beats a drum. Waves cymbal-crash. The willy-willy wind whirls our feather bodies. Our coats spinnaker as we float weightless, defying gravity.

Wind blows out banksia flower candles. It runs its fingers through my hair, breathes down my neck and whispers sweet nothings in my ear. I close my eyes to a symphony of sounds. A thrush tunes up. Thornbills practise their scales. Wind whistles through piccolo tea-tree. It plucks out notes on spider web strings. The metronome sea keeps time. When I open my eyes the forest is dancing. Saplings sway. Banksia flowers pirouette and fall giddy on the ground.

On mild days I sit on the steps and catch the sun. Light-fingered rays stroke my eyelids. Warm air tickles my cheeks. Bee-hum wakes me. It's hard to believe that at seven this morning we shivered over the stove. Teasing out a few weeds jammed between stones is a cure for winter blues. Rubbing flannel lamb's ear between my fingers feels pyjama-soft.

Labour is heavier. We lug loads of wood and dump them on the woodheap by the sawhorse. We ferret round the tip for rotted fence posts and palings, grubbed-out stumps and off-cuts. We swing the axe, split kindling and stack bundles on the back verandah. The chainsaw screams through the bush, spitting sawdust and making a meal of a dead tree.

Nights can be bitter. We scrunch up newspaper, drag in dead branches and twigs and crack kindling against our knees. We huff and puff our cheeks to bellow air. Sparks glow. Paper fans flames. We rub our hands together and stare into the blaze. We poke sticks at crumbly banksia logs spitting and crackling red and purple against firebricks blackened by so many fires.

I reflect on the day, years ago, when we visited Jean Galbraith, colleague of Edna Walling, at her Gippsland home, Dunedin, near Tyers. We chatted by the winter fire, sipping raspberry vinegar in her old-world lounge room. Her writing table was stacked with journals and books. Paintings and photographs covered the walls. I counted fourteen vases and jars crammed with flowers. A window framed a garden wonderland that echoed her long lifetime. We watched a black satin bowerbird's whirring display as he danced around a twiggy nest decorated with blue biros, plastic straws, bottle tops and clothes pegs.

Jean made an impression on me. But it wasn't her awesome knowledge as author, botanist and conservationist or even her memorable garden. Her warmth and sense of calm touched me. Her eyes radiated joy. She balanced exotic and native flora in her aesthetic lifestyle. Only years after meeting her, corresponding with her and reading her books I realised her influence on my holistic approach to the garden and the broader picture of the natural world around me.

Back home, we sit in silence. Spuds roast in charred jackets. Cheese sizzles in the jaffle iron. We toast our legs and cook up ideas. Projects simmer. The kettle boils dry. We nod off. Flames die down to a sprinkle of coals. At bedtime we are sleepy dreamers, rockabyed, lullabyed and hushabyed by the sea.

Some cold-blooded nights we brave a campfire. Seabirds coo on the Inlet. Constellations pinprick the sky. Away from town, skies are stargazing clear. Stars shiver, silver, red and blue, flashing rubies and sapphires scattered across black velvet. On moonless nights, lantern-bright stars guide us along familiar paths. Eyes as radiant as supernovas, the kids gaze up connecting a celestial dot-to-dot saucepan or Southern Cross. A shooting star smudges the sky.

Shadows flicker through the banksias. Sparks shoot up. Hot coals pop like penny bungers on cracker night. The fire links me with the spirit of the Bunurong. Family groups roamed the coast west of the Tarwin River twenty thousand years ago. The Aboriginal people worked in harmony with local plants, gathering manna from gums and foraging for seeds, leaves, grasses, roots, fungi and honey. The Bunurong made camp here, cooking kangaroo, sharing mussels and pipis collected from the ocean's larder, harvesting rock pools, beach estuaries and coastal plains. Kitchen middens crackle with gritty remains of bones and shells still flecked through the Venus Bay dunes.

Ghost voices mutter stories. I hear songs and the mesmerising rhythm of tapping-sticks. Sinewy bodies dance in the ring of firelight. I can feel the vibration of feet drumming on the ground. We are intruders with pale skin and no black blood in our veins, but tonight we share the Kooris' hearth and dreamtime.

Fig damper cooks in a rust-crusted camp oven. I hook a stick under the handle and drag it through the ash. Flames die down. A log smoulders. Voices hush. Shadowed faces soften. We squat on our haunches and sip hot tea, huddling close with our backs to the wind, listening to owls calling, the stumpy legs of a wombat's gallop, and the kettle hissing in the embers.

Morning sky is as blank as a blackboard. Wind erases chalky cloud. Drops sprinkle the roof. Rain sets in. A crow cries. Kangaroos thump onto the verandah. The house shudders. The open fire flickers like flares. It comes to our rescue and keeps spirits afloat.

A ground thrush stands statue-stiff pretending he's invisible. His dawn flute-warble only adds to his charm. Birdsong volume is turned down low. Crickets have quietened.

The butcherbird's mellow, piping song is deceptive. He is a serial killer, slaughtering silver eyes, thornbills, small mammals and reptiles. He lies low in tea-tree, arrows from nowhere, stabs a blue-wren, pins it to the fork of a tree and carries it by the scruff of its neck back to his tree house. His hooked beak hangs the carcass around a cup-and-saucer nest. A rollicking alarm shrieks through the forest, warning small birds to take cover.

A fox, scavenging a dead gull or rotten fish, footprints the shore. Daytime foxes telltale cold weather. We make split-second eye contact. His fur coat glows russet red against tea-tree trunks. Paws barely touch the forest floor as he gives me the slip and vanishes.

In the dead of night a cough wakes me. A fox is out on the prowl, sniffing at the wind and doing his rounds. My fingers feel for the torch, flick the switch and I stumble up to the garden. In the bat-black night the light casts distorted shadows. A possum shakes a banksia branch. A moonlit tawny frogmouth spooks me. His camouflage is clever. Slit yellow eyes, streaky-grey mottled wings and tufted head feathers that resemble bushy eyebrows. Poised to swoop a moth or spider, he plays dead and tries to pass himself off as a bit of wood. The slip bolt rattles. Mice scuttle off. Hens purr on their perches and ignore the intrusion. I shut off the light. I can hear flesh tearing and smell the stink of blood soaking the night air.

Feral cats are lone wolves, out night hunting in the leaner months. They are dumpier than their sleeker, domestic feline brothers and sisters. The cats are cagey and skilful at avoiding people. Clues of scattered feathers and make-your-skin-crawl whines warn of their bloodshed. Cats claw at my concern for possums, frogs, lizards and nesting seabirds. But to catch a cat takes cunning and persistence. Saucers of supper and purring 'puss, puss, puss' in the dark only might make a cat enter a cage. Seduced by something fishy hooked onto a trip-wire, the trapdoor slams. We have no mercy.

A bird of prey circles above the chook run one afternoon. Its black silhouette, underwing pattern, fingered wing tip and diamond-shaped tail distinguish it from similar hawks. It's an adult male wedge-tailed eagle. I imagine taloned feet hooking into a bantam and hauling it off to a feeding platform to extend its menu of mammals, reptiles and birds, but after casing the joint he glides off as quietly as he came.

The wind's husky voice calls me. Trees shiver against asphalt skies. Rain-washed greens glow. Wet branches whip my face. The landscape is lit with torch blossoms. Wattles flush sulphur-yellow. Branches are weighed with gold. Tracks are paved in gold dust. Heath perfume floods the forest. A web-trapped star flower sparkles. Galaxies of fallen flowers mimic an earthen Milky Way. In the hairy-headed dunes, pig-face leaves glisten in frail sunlight.

Winter reaches a stalemate. Sullen skies mourn the loss of a bright-eyed sun. Whingeing winds keep me captive in the kitchen. Winter's tail end stretches out like a prison sentence. I feel as if I'm doing time in solitary confinement, counting the not-long-to-go-now days until spring shows its face. I curl up by the wood stove like a bulb waiting to come up or a seed ready to sprout.

Bad habits wear out winter's welcome. It lags behind and weakens its grip. It wrings wet hands and the last drops drip away.

MUDBRICK AND STONE

Mudbrick offered an alternative to the pop-ups and pre-fabs, fibro and hardiplank houses scattered along the coastline. It reflected the textures of the bush. Its timeless quality, earthy aesthetics, flexibility to design, insulation against heat and cold, fire resistance and low cost were irresistible. Its hands-on, do-it-yourself construction won us over.

The tools of the trade were basic: wheelbarrow, shovel, bucket, trowel, spirit level, mallet and chisel. Clay was trucked in from the local Koonwarra quarry. We rolled up our sleeves, spat on our hands and got stuck into it.

We skidded through puddles, ramming earth, pressing out brick after brick as if on an assembly line. We worked like zombies to the click-clack of the hand-operated press. We stacked sun-baked blocks stairway-high. Grains of grit stuck between our teeth and split our fingernails. Clay clogged our ears, stung our cuts, splattered our faces and plastered our clothes until we resembled statues dug from some lost civilisation.

A slab was poured. The bones of a post-and-beam ribcage were fleshed out with earth. Bucket loads of mortar balanced on a plank wedged between two ladders as we hurled on mud and braided in the brick-weave pattern. We didn't need the skill of artisans. Craftsmanship came from commonsense and attention to detail.

We hunted around for throw-outs. Timber was salvaged from the Foster pub. We scrounged bricks from the Dumbalk butter factory and doors from the Pine Lodge guesthouse at Inverloch. Sets of windows were scored for ten bucks the lot. These second-hand materials felt like hand-me-downs from elderly relatives who had passed away. But like picking off lint from an old woollen jumper, the time-worn materials needed sprucing up.

We chipped mortar from bricks and puttied window frames. We scraped shellac, yanked out nails with a pinch bar and peeled off paint decades thick. Acid baths stripped wood raw. We screwed up our faces to the stink of caustic soda fumes. We scrubbed down and sanded back, rubbed linseed oil into cedar and polished pine with beeswax. The grainy timbers came to life. Granite glass doors filtered shell-pink and kelp-green light into bedrooms. On warm days, french doors were flung open to the bush.

We moved in. The yard was stacked with spare parts for the house. Just-in-case timber, a ready-when-you-are cement trough and claw-foot bath stood under scrap iron. The house resembled a demolition site. Black plastic flapped on window gaps. Sheets of tin were tacked across doorways. It was rough-and-ready down-market. We couldn't care less. We were home. We bunged up cracks with Polyfilla and scraped and rubbed and rendered. We sealed and slapped on 'missed a bit' and 'needs another coat' white paint-skin.

The walls are not even. When you run your fingers along

them they don't feel plaster smooth but lumpy with quartz and clay, gravel and grass and bits of leaves. They are pressed with kids' palm prints, dented with heel marks and boot prints. Individual bricks are chipped, stuck with hair strands, broken thumbnails and smudged with fingerprints. It took one whole year, but from a pile of clay we had sculpted a home.

The house settled in. In time it floated on a tea-tree sea. The ship funnel chimney chugged out smoke. On stormy days when the furnace was stoked, it was full steam ahead.

Stone seduced us. Its amber, almond and slate-grey tones blended with the landscape. Its mellow, weathered texture complemented the folky architecture and garden style. Its step-back-in-time beauty and endless functional possibilities took hold.

We were old hands. We'd built a whole house. A wall would be a pushover. Or so we thought. Mudbrick is uniform and pliable. Rows are repetitive. But rock is heavy. It's brittle. Each one differs. Stone walling is slow. It takes time. It's hard yakka. Spatial problems of scale and pattern need to be solved. It's a cut-to-size three-dimensional jigsaw.

The key to a strong wall is not mortar but care to lock each stone in place. Aesthetic results come from eye-hand skill, a love of the material and judging the quality of individual stones. Potential crook backs, dicky knees, cricks-in-the-neck, slipped discs and smashed-to-smithereens big toes made safety-with-stone and steel-capped boots a good idea.

One wall and we were addicted. We left no stone unturned. Piles of rubble transformed to paths, retaining and freestanding walls, steps, seats, duck house, conservatory and a chimney stack in the cottage.

We dug back in time with a pinch bar and prised out history.

We stone-masoned steps in Machu Pichu, friezes and frescoes in Florence. We carved colonnades in Constantinople and pillars in the Parthenon. Visitors asked, 'Were the walls built by convict labour?' We nodded.

Each stone was hand picked. From a quarry forty kilometres away we lugged slabs of basalt onto the ute till it sagged under the strain. We hauled load after load. We stockpiled. Stone by stone we stacked and sorted. Flat ones for paving. Whoppers for footings. Narrow ones for edging. Tumblings of rock echoed an archaeological dig.

The bush rang with the chink of chisel on stone. Flints flew. Rock broken-to-fit split in two or shattered to rubble. Our hands, clothes and boots were spattered with dust that dried our throats and reddened our eyes. The smoke-ash smell clogged our nostrils. We spat and wheezed and worked up a sweat, grunted and groaned and cursed. We jammed our fingers, scraped our knuckles and stubbed our toes. Arm muscles bulged as we dragged stones up hill, flipped them down hill and wheeled them along on their edges. We balanced knee-trembler slabs on the crowbar and wriggled them easy-does-it into place. We wobbled under the weight till our legs gave out. We fell in a heap at smoko. Flaked at arvo tea. At night we hobbled bone-tired into gravel-grained sheets and slept like the dead.

Paths vein the garden. Walls relieve flat ground and double as seating. Sand slips through your fingers but stone is for keeps. It comes with a lifetime guarantee. It has given the garden a rock-solid foundation. We still find excuses to use it.

VEGETABLE GARDEN

My earliest memory is from a vegetable garden. Gripping the 'reins' of Dad's jumper, I skipped behind him between rows of cabbages and silver beet. Strawberries spilled from an earth-filled enamel tub rescued from our old washing machine. I learned at the feet of my father as he raked in radish seed and pinched off tomato shoots.

When the milko's horse clopped down our road, Dad (like many dads in the 1950s) dashed out, scraped a shovel along the asphalt and scooped up steamy lumps of manure. He raced down to the vegie patch, balancing the shovel like a giant egg and spoon. My father sowed the seed for my future love of growing vegies.

Terry and I started with a vegetable garden, but we had no proper plan. We didn't contemplate the site; didn't observe where shadows were cast, note the arc of the sun's path, hot spots or wind patterns. We made it up as we went along. It came together bit by bit. In the backs of our minds we had a vague notion of feed-the-family self-sufficiency, but at first we just intended to grow some fruit trees and a few tomatoes.

By building our own home in the bush and planting seeds for food, we were following in the footsteps of the Gippsland pioneers. I felt an affinity with the early settlers. In 1801, Lieutenant John Grant planted South Gippsland and Victoria's first garden at Churchill Island near Phillip Island. Grant wrote in his journal:

> *I sowed several sorts of seeds, together with wheat, Indian corn, peas ... and I did not forget to plant potatoes ...*
>
> *I planted the stones and kernels of several fruits I had brought out, not forgetting that of the curious apple.*

This garden produced the first harvestable wheat crop in Victoria.

I bit my bottom lip. Starting from scratch was a big ask. We had to face the facts. The wind pounded. The sand was so dry it poured through my fist. We had no watering system. We were gardening against the odds.

But the patch had some redeeming features. It faced north. Wrap-around forest modified gales and gave some protection. Though in bad-tempered winds we heard banksia limbs groaning, branches snapping and the crack of tea-tree splitting in two, we had an instant walled garden. The rough space had possibilities.

In the clearing I mattocked bracken stubs and levelled out rabbit warrens. I kicked at the dirt with my boots, dragged a stick through the dust and scratched out a circle. The scarifier cut through the earth's skin like fingernails. I dug up buried bones: kangaroo teeth, a wombat skull and the broken wings of a pipi shell. I hit a problem. I was in two minds about changing a landscape. Exotic plants in native bushland had moral implications. There was a culture clash. Pangs of guilt moved through me. Gippsland may have grown the first wheat crop but somehow a contemporary bush garden went against the grain.

I considered Edna Walling's sensitive incorporation of exotics with natives. I took heed of Peter Cuffley's words from *Cottage Gardens in Australia* on 'the intelligent approach to created gardens and the natural environment', where he states:

> *I find it difficult to bear the puritanical approach for created gardens where no foreign element is allowed to appear ...*
>
> *... wherever people create gardens they have choices and hopefully such choices will be not only well informed but inspired.*

This is not virgin bush. It has regenerated after years of cattle farming. We would find middle ground. With care and commitment we were confident we could balance a garden with a delicate coastal environment.

We set ground rules. The garden would be restricted to a quarter hectare. It would be fenced. We were aware of the consequences of environmental weeds in the bush. Potential weeds would be avoided. Tearaways that might jump the fence would be dealt with. Search-and-destroy missions would weed out ragwort. We would preserve the native vegetation. We would have no domestic animals, cats or dogs that could disturb the wildlife. We had bought seven hectares of land but deep down we knew we were custodians with a responsibility.

We pegged out a twenty-metre square plot. No graders roared in. No bulldozers. No front-end loaders. Earth was moved manually; levelled by hand and hoe, shovel and rake, string line and eye line. I raked in leaf litter and chicken manure. I flicked out fistfuls of seeds, pressed my palms in the dust, watered and waited with fingers crossed.

Nothing came up. I could take a hint. This wasn't going to be easy. Weeks later, I tried again. A few weeds and scrawny sunflowers straggled up to the light. The crude little garden struggled. Unfenced, it was a free feed for rabbits and wildlife. It was exposed to winds that whipped the plants to shreds. Buckets of water were sloshed up from the house tank but it was like watering a sieve.

Sand is lean and hungry. It dries out quickly and needs constant topping up to come up with the goods. The saying 'Clay will break your back but sand will break your heart' hit a nerve. But there was an up side: sand drains well. It's aerated. It warms up quickly after winter. The spade slips through it with suspicious ease. It has potential. Compost gives sand a pulse and can transform it into a friable fertile loam alive with micro-organisms and rippling with soil-ploughing earthworms.

There was no choice. It was all or nothing. Either we improved the soil or we wouldn't have fresh food. We made compost; nothing beats it as a works-wonders fertiliser. We sniffed out manure sources, tracked down cattle yards and sheep sheds, mucked out stables and haysheds, pig pens and poultry farms. We picked up cow pats from paddocks. We carted truckloads of spoiled hay, pitch-forked urine-soaked straw, gathered seaweed and garbage bags lumpy with leaves from the tip. Friends asked, 'What's the best mulch?' We answered, 'Anything you can get your hands on.'

We pinched our noses to plug the pong. We scraped out sheep manure flecked with scrags and thick with blowies. Pig poo stuck on our boot soles. Sheep dust rubbed its way in to our socks and hair. We were up to our necks in it. But the manure crumbled to rich, dark, sweet-smelling loam. Liquid clay gave the sand backbone. We soaked raw clay in water till it was sloppy then poured it around the vegetables. Good soil was half the battle.

We had presumed the coast was frost-free. Wrong. Frost glazed our first winter garden. It burned tamarillos black and gnawed at heliotrope. On chilled mornings the beds lay like mummies shrouded in white sheets. In spring we moved the frost-tender to sheltered spots.

We filched ideas. Eyes peeled, we snooped down suburban streets and poked our noses over front fences. We gave one another a leg-up and sticky-beaked into backyards. We picked the brains of fully fledged gardeners in the know. We twisted the arm of an expert (our Italian friend Paolo who knew a thing or two) till he spilled the beans and set us straight. We learned on the job: a crash course in outdoor education. At night we did our homework. Heads down, we studied the syllabus. We read up on root crops, mildew and collar rot until we knew it off by heart. Would we romp it in or bomb out badly ? Summer would mark our exam paper.

I began a journal in an out-of-date diary. It became a written think-tank, a Self-Help-How-to-Succeed and a Beginner's Guide to Gardening-Made-Easy. I plagiarised, copied and adapted. I cut-and-pasted photos and tore pictures from magazines. I wrote reminders on tea-stained pages. I ticked off and crossed out; underlined what worked and deleted the duds. I pencilled in rough sketches and scribbled in midnight brainwaves. I listed memos, warnings and instructions to myself under headings: 'Bits to Fix Up' and 'Stuff to Do'. I jotted down pearls of wisdom about the whole gardening experience: 'Gardening is eleven months of hard work and one month of disappointment'. In all the chaos the bits began to fall into place.

We mapped out a mental plan. We experimented. Too-early tomatoes were trialed in plastic tepees. Seaweed soaked in forty-four gallon drums. Out-of-season spuds spilled from piled-up retreads. A chamomile lawn crept across broken-brick paving. Strawberries were set in rat boobytraps for blackbirds (not recommended). The tip was a one-stop shop. Scrap timber for box beds. Newspapers for mulch. A cracked window to cover a cold frame. Carpet scraps to smother weeds. We followed fads. Raised beds. Double-dig. No-dig. We were slow on the uptake but it didn't take much to work out that 'organic' was the way to go. We planted by the phases of the moon. Leafy crops on the waxing moon and root crops on the waning moon. While we didn't notice a marked difference in seed germination, we felt in tune with the cycles of the moon, its affect on the tides and the forces of the natural world around us.

There were a few hitches. Rabbits wangled their way in. We never did have enough compost, but we were on the right track. Still finding our feet, we bumbled our way to success. We learned that the soil is the garden's heartbeat. Compost gave it a new lease of life. We mulched with whatever was at hand and whatever we could scrounge: newspapers, cardboard, seaweed, sawdust, wood chips, rice hulls, spoiled hay and manures. We dusted on dolomite and handfuls of blood and bone. In sheltered hotspots small cantaloupes and watermelons made their way down wormy mounds. We were just following the basic rules of good garden practice but we felt we'd found the secret to a succession of organically grown vegetables, fruits and flowers.

The vegie garden took off. But it was shapeless. It needed a new image. Well-dressed gardens were wearing potagers. We followed the fashion, tailoring it to suit our needs. It was revamped into patterned beds that were all the go. It was not tape-measured. Lines were not ruler-straight. More by untrained eye and rule of thumb. Paced out by footsteps, arm-lengths and hand-spans. Brick-stone paths, wide enough for a wheelbarrow, divided beds.

Borders were trimmed with suitably dressed plants that though imported, did not brag pricey labels. We chose long-lasting, hard-wearing fabrics. Heavy-duty rosemary and dwarf English lavenders Hidcote and Munstead would stand up to the wear-and-tear of dry summers and sandy soil and look tres chic to boot.

We worked on a shoestring budget. Materials were pre-loved or dirt cheap. Broken bricks were scrounged from friends. Reclaimed timbers were scrubbed up good as new. Stone was bought at rock-bottom prices. To echo the buildings' rooflines Terry crafted four obelisks for next to nothing. We bluffed our way to making the garden appear as if it had been designed from the beginning.

Ornamental food gardens supply a feast for the table and for the eyes. This structured style of kitchen garden is decorative, easy to organise and space saving. But a potager needs upkeep. Tending and grooming are part of the process. Growing a range of vegetables is labour-intensive. Leafy greens have a short lifespan. Planting is ongoing. This is a working garden.

I am not a slave to symmetry. There is no grid system. Paths are crooked. Beds are irregular. Rows are uneven. Patterns are not precise. It's not spick and span. It's not weed-free. There are gaps and overcrowding. Seeding vegetables are untidy but loosen formality and save work.

We sow non-hybrid seeds: open-pollinated varieties that self-seed true to type. We collect and swap seeds with friends to help ensure that these older varieties are not lost. Phoenix Seeds (P.O. Snug, 7054 Tasmania) has a catalogue boasting a wide range of organically grown heritage and non-hybrid varieties.

Constant mulching and dense planting cuts down weeding and

watering. Perennial red currants, raspberries and rhubarb, strawberries, asparagus and artichokes keep the area brimming with goodies. Culinary herbs, basil, borage, dill, caraway, coriander, thyme, oregano, tarragon, marigolds and nasturtiums fill the gaps, deter pests and add colour, shape, texture, pattern and a smorgasbord of scents.

We got the hang of it. We rolled into a rhythm: spreading compost, sowing seeds and willing them to sprout, firming in seedlings and coaxing them to swell, splashing on water, stooping, squatting on our haunches, filling the weeding basket, luring lettuces to have a heart, tying canes with twine and tomato vines to a wigwam of sticks, heaping up soil around the corn, twisting cucumber tendrils onto latticework, handcuffing the thin wrists of espaliered trees to the fence, binding up parcels of oatgrass, scanning for slugs, taking pot-shots at blackbirds, shooing chooks, cursing rabbits, stalking wombats, kangaroo control and sometimes even picking, it all began to flow into part of the cycle. Rather than menial chores, the tasks have come to be a kind of outdoor housework (always preferable to the indoor variety) enjoyed as day-to-day rituals.

It's easy to lose myself, thoughts drifting, thinking out loud, wandering the paths with a faraway look in my eyes; effortlessly snipping off a butter bean here, a snow pea there, pinching a raspberry, rubbing a basil leaf, nibbling on a parsley stalk; sniffing lemon thyme, brushing my hand across the rosemary hedge; watching a skink scale a wall or feel one flicker up my arm, contemplating whatever springs to mind or absolutely nothing. I splash the spinach and watch quicksilver slide down nasturtium leaves. I stray with the sticky weed and mingle with the marrows. I chat to the chicory, pat cabbages on the head and marvel, 'My, how you've grown.' Hours slip by though the time seems only minutes.

Planning through the seasons keeps the vegies going all year. We keep seed trays full and stay one step ahead. As crop use-by dates expire, back-up seedlings and follow-up planting make sure the storeroom is stacked.

A living pantry is more than convenient. Out in the sticks it's a luxury. A garden that never shuts up shop means not being caught short for ingredients. The cupboard is barer in winter. Rains can cut supplies. Winds can drive a hard bargain. Sun can cause a sell out. Hail can cancel the order. Some seasons just don't come up with the goods. Shelf life can be short. Items can be discontinued. You can be hard-pressed to rustle up the makings for a meal. Available only while stocks last. But you never come home empty-handed.

It's a take-away trip to your own private greengrocer's. Open all hours. All you can eat. It's fresher than a street market. More therapeutic than retail therapy. Even if you are just browsing or window-shopping, you get to try-as-you-buy: slurp a peach, crunch a carrot or tuck your teeth into a tomato. You get to maul the merchandise: fondle the fennel, grope a gourd or smack the bottoms of pumpkins. With pat-yourself-on-the-back satisfaction you get to tick off a long shopping-spree list of vegies: asparagus peas, kohlrabi, okra, orach, sea kale, salsify and shungiku that don't stretch the household budget. No queues. No waiting. No charge. It's hard to beat a heaped-up hamper or shirt/skirt carry-bag of goodies delivered to the doorstep. It's flavour-of-the-month all year. The seasons decide what's on the menu. Instant meals in minutes.

The potager is a tapestry of colour, shape and texture. Secateurs are scissors snipping twine. My gloves are a thimble for every finger. My trowel is a needle glinting in the sun. I sew on corn seeds and pull a thread of seedlings through the soil. I plant in patterns, weave with flowers and herringbone with herbs. I cross-stitch with cabbages, crochet lace with lettuces and zigzag with zucchinis. Fennel forms a foil for artichokes. Steel-blue broccoli clash with carrots. Chives overlap parsley.

Mother Nature lends a hand. Her sewing box is crammed with spools and skeins, cottons and yarns, reels of ribbon, bobbins and buttons, beetles and butterflies, bee-sting and cactus pins. She pricks her finger, puckers and pleats, folds and smocks and crimps leaves with serrated shears. She stitches with ants, embroiders with webs and sequins with dew. She sun-spins gold thread. She beads with seeds, hail-pearls, raindrops and apples, looping and linking, pushing in and pulling out.

I stroke her handiwork. Rub fabrics between my fingers. Homespun linen, velvet, wool, crepe and crimplene, cotton, felt and gauzy chiffon. She sun-splashes and shades. Adds birdsong and scent. She breathes a sea breeze through the loose-weave, humming a sea song, darning holes by the light-bulb moon. She is a magical seamstress.

Summer turns to autumn. Threads unravel. Seams come apart. Invisible stitching is unpicked. Hems are mended. Loose ends are trimmed and tied.

With the passage of the seasons the vegetable garden shifts. The bush house is a good spot to take a breather and gather my thoughts when the light is fading in the late afternoon. I squint through the needle's eye to the tapestry of the gourmet garden. Silver artichokes and lavenders tone in with the smoky backdrop. The edible landscapes' patterns contrast with the bush.

Spring

After winter's starchier flavours, craved-for dishes of crunchy snow peas, baby broad beans steamed whole in their skins, fist-sized artichoke hearts and asparagus tips wake taste buds to the season's treats.

Autumn's groundwork revives the vegetable garden. Compost collapses to one third of its original bulk. I slip my palm under the quilt of hessian sacking, carpet underfelt and soggy straw pillows crawling with slaters. My fingers are gloved in the fluffy warmth. I peel off the covers teeming with leaping black critters.

Top layers are moist, plum-pudding dark and semi-decayed. But down in the underworld, coffee-coloured loam smells mould-sweet. Ribboned with worms, it crumbles between my fingers. I am a miner for treasure as I plunge in the pitchfork, fill the barrow and stagger up to the garden. I top-dress the vegetables, roses and perennials, boosting them for the growing spell ahead.

As days lengthen my interest sharpens. Sun oils my joints. My fingers wiggle like root fibres ready to spread. In the potting shed I wade through sacks and stacks of hair-cracked pots, rusty hoe heads, a three-teethed rake in need of dental work and wads of fly-specked newspapers powdered with potting mix and rat droppings. Makeshift shelves are sticky with cobwebs and crammed with curling packets. I check my stash. Success with seeds can be hit-and-miss, but a packet of seeds holds hope.

Seeds are jammed into ribbed-glass coffee jars and jam jars scrawled with texta, part deciphered, part remembered as Lazy Housewife beans. Seeds have been tucked into biscuit tins, stuffed into shoeboxes and crammed into drawers. Folded envelopes scatter unidentifiable dust. Black specks shower from paper bags. Streams of seeds spill across the table: wooden button broad beans, translucent beads of corn seed, burred carrot, winged-veined discs of parsnip seeds, gravel-rough silver beet seeds, kidney-shaped bean seeds, furry tomato seeds, sunflower seeds dressed in pin-striped suits. Shake, rattle and roll.

The rough-cut table is caked with river sand. It's cluttered with plastic trays, a bent-back trowel and chipped clay pots. I swirl and tap the half-filled sieve. It jiggles with gravel and grit, showering a dark dust that drifts across trays dotted with lettuce, tomato, capsicum, cucumber, marigold and nasturtium seeds. I squeeze the trigger of the spray bottle, puffing out a milky mist. If they survive mice and mould, the sun-warmed seeds will swell to green bumps, and just when my back's turned, they will unfold to the silent miracle of a plant. Sowings are staggered. Pricked out seedlings will provide bundles of vegetables and salad greens for summer.

But I have been caught out. Too busy, too disorganised or just too darned lazy to get seeds in on time. And at a cost. It's a forty-kilometre trip to the supermarket for over-priced seedlings or vegetables that don't make the grade. No pumpkins or potatoes and winter's larder near empty. No sweet corn and summer's not the same. No spring parsley and I go pale. No autumn-dug garlic and life's hardly worth living. Slacking off from just a few minutes' work means missing out on vegies that make or break the menu.

The soil warms up but nights can be wintry. Spring plays the trickster. Now-you-see-it, now-you-don't, then it's coming-ready-or-not. Spring has a short attention span. One minute all sweetness and light, the next it throws a tantrum around the equinox. Spring changes its mind and refuses to cooperate, shakes a fist and stamps its feet, storms off in a huff, flattens and shreds crops. Spring makes no promises and gives nothing away. It forges its signature across fine days and hoodwinks us to believe they're here to stay. Late frosts caution against planting out zucchinis and tomatoes. When I get to know it better, spring gives me the nod, a wink or a wave when it's time to get cracking.

The gate latch clicks as I stride up the orchard's stone steps. My skirt hem brushes flowering thyme. I am swept along by the fresh smells after last night's showers. The landscape is lit by morning sun. Bees dance to the trills, pipings, warbles, squeaks and whip cracks of birdsong. It's eight in the morning and bees are blind drunk, swaggering from cup to cup, working the pub-crawl pollen from apple, pear, quince, tea-tree and broad bean blossoms. Eye-high spinach flowers confetti down. Asparagus spears glint like steel as they cut through the warm soil. Artichokes are set in sterling silver. I tear off a few damp broad beans.

Podding fur-lined shells for thumbnail-sized beans is a tasty launch into harvesting spring vegetables. Finger-sized beans still tucked in their pods are steamed with mint and eaten skin and all. Coles Dwarf is more resilient to wind hammerings here than the taller varieties, though even these beans are walloped when they are ready around October. Broad beans crop even better in these poor soils. Whoppers are left to shrivel on the plant for seeds. When the beans die off I slash the stems to the ground so root nodules will charge the soil for follow-up brassica crops.

Popping just-picked pea pods has nostalgic memories. A colander in my lap, peas ping-ponging into a saucepan is my pea-growing fantasy. But as soon as the curly white flowers form pods, they are snatched, stripped and eaten raw by children and rabbits. Few peas make it to the table for meals.

Asparagus is a harbinger of spring. It's one of the earliest cultivated vegetables. Barrow loads of manure and spoiled straw supply green-tipped spears from September till December. I plunge string-tied bunches into boiling water, blanche and serve with a simple dressing of virgin olive oil, lemon juice, cracked peppercorns and a few flakes of sea salt.

Jagged silver artichoke leaves add architectural impact but they need elbow room. Cobalt-blue flowers are a bonus before thistledown sets sail in summer winds. I head hunt and cut the throats of two varieties. Dull-green blunt fruits crop from August to November. Streaky, purple-hued artichokes are ready from September to November. Earwigs bury themselves between leaves but crawl off when the heads are bashed together and rinsed. Outer leaves are stripped to get to the heart. The artichokes are sautéed, steamed, stuffed, fried, roasted, char-grilled and pickled. One of my favourite artichoke dishes is the Italian cariciofo paste.

Artichoke Paste

Choose small but plump artichokes. Trim off outer leaves. Toss into a bowl of water to which slices of lemon have been added to prevent discolouring. Drop artichoke hearts in salted boiling water and cook until centre-soft. This takes about ten minutes depending on size. Drain. Transfer to blender or pestle and mortar. To four artichokes dribble in approximately one hundred mls of extra virgin olive oil, one to two crushed garlic bulbs, a good squeeze of lemon juice, salt and cracked black pepper. Blend into a cream-smooth paste.

I serve this with crusty ciabata or bread sticks sprinkled with rosemary and a glass of red. Bellissimo.

As the weather warms, pests appear from nowhere. I steer clear of spraying. Pesticides kill insect predators that keep the balance. Pests are kept under the thumb by rotating crops and improving the soil. Layers of compost and mulch are continually shovelled on and raked over. This invites a wriggling worm population that bumps up bird numbers. The birds keep bugs at bay. Blue-tongue lizards and blue wrens, yellow robins, firetails and thornbills feed on a diet of tatty-winged cabbage moths. Silver eyes and ladybirds dine on sap suckers and rosebuds sticky with aphids. I always keep a watchful eye for pests that can be 'nipped in the bud'. I circle sawdust around young blackjack and butterfingered zucchini, pumpkin, lettuce and capsicum seedlings to slow down the slugs. Snail pellets are sprinkled as a last resort when all else fails.

Armed and dangerous, I flick caterpillars, crush creepy-crawlies, squirt mildew with the hose, squash aphids, stamp on slugs, slimies and slipperies and smash snails with the heel of my boot. In the dead of night, wombats bulldoze under the fence. Rabbits cash in on the easy pickings, digging holes, hilling-up droppings and gnawing brassicas to stumps.

Blackbirds scratch up seeds and seedlings and flick mulch onto paths. Junkyard sculpture is knitted together from odds and ends on bits of string. Broken mirrors and ring-pull tops flicker in the sun. Trinkets tinkle in the wind. These scare tactics put the birds off only for a while.

Duck quacks echo through the garden. I grab a loaf of day-old bread and crunch through weedy gravel to set them free. A squall whirls in from nowhere as I mutter a 'Good morning, girls' greeting. The ducks are on the loose, snatching the torn bread from my hand before waddling off to work over the vegie garden. Bills burrow for slugs and snap at insects. Ducks prefer to tear at prickly plants, especially borage and comfrey, and cause little damage to the leafy vegetables, though our girls are partial to silver beet.

Ducks are stout-hearted and long-lived. The Pekins and Khaki-Campbells are endearing, quirky characters, bred for eggs rather than meat. Inside their house, a straw nest is decorated with five mud-splattered eggs. In the kitchen the shells are shiny when scrubbed under running water. The fresh eggs are heavy, orange-yolked, strong-flavoured and will add extra richness to custards and cakes.

This moist cake is a family favourite. My son Jarrah throws it together if he's hungry enough. It eases early summer's zucchini overload.

Zucchini and Walnut Cake

2 cups self-raising flour

1 cup sugar

1 teaspoon cinnamon

1 cup sunflower oil

3 eggs

2 cups grated zucchini

1 cup walnuts

1 teaspoon vanilla essence or brandy

Cream Cheese Icing

Blend 125 grams of cream cheese with 250 grams of pure icing sugar, 50 grams of softened butter and a squeeze of lemon juice. Sprinkle walnuts on top.

Mix flour, sugar and spice together. Beat in oil and eggs. Stir in zucchini and walnuts. Add vanilla. Pour mixture into oiled tin and bake in a moderate oven (180°C) for about an hour. When cool, dust with icing sugar or spread with cream cheese icing. Hard to resist.

The chooks start to lay again. Breakfast is a mish-mash of toast crusts and porridge. I disturb a clucky bantam from her cosy nest. She mumbles under her breath as I collect three warm brown eggs and place them in the makeshift pouch of my shirt.

Each egg becomes like the chook's own handwriting, recognised by its particular shape, colour and size.

We have enjoyed many different breeds of poultry over the years; Black Orpington, Rhode Island Red, New Hampshire, Leghorn and Wyandotte, but my best loved is the Ancona. Vivid red comb and wattle set off black-speckled white feathers. Anconas have a fiesty Italian temperament. Slight frames give leave to flighty escapes from the coop. On the steps, my pet hen Dotty squats on my lap and nuzzles in for a stroke of her feathers. Her beak tickles the palm of my cupped hand as she pecks a nest of oatmeal, wobbles her wattles and then flaps off to freedom. Back in the kitchen I crack the eggs into a flour well and mix dough for cutting into pasta ribbons.

Easy Home-Made Pasta

4 cups plain flour
6 small or 4 large fresh eggs
good pinch of salt

Mix ingredients together and knead. Leave covered dough for at least half an hour at room temperature. Cut dough in half. Sprinkle on extra flour if too sticky. Roll through pasta machine on low setting. Continue on higher setting. Pass through cutter setting for strips of fettucini. Cook in boiling water for a couple of minutes. Drain. Serves four.

Ravioli

Place narrow sheets of pasta dough on floured bench. Spoon on spaced fillings. (My current favourites are spinach, thyme and goat's cheese and pureed pumpkin, parmesan cheese, sage and mushroom.) Brush edges with egg white or water. Cover with a top sheet. Firmly press edges between each spoonful. Cut with pastry wheel into pillows. Cook briefly in boiling water. Serve with basil and home-made tomato sauce. Sprinkle with grated parmesan.

Despite all the mulch, the garden drowns in a wave of weeds. Catching them as seedlings, preferably after rain and before they set seed and roots develop, saves hours of work. On a mission, I march into combat. It can be a losing battle. Milk thistles, mallow, capeweed and oatgrass lift easily, pulled by hand, but sticky weed is unstoppable. It grabs me from behind. It gets calendula in its clutches and spinach in a stranglehold. Low-life couch grass can't be trusted. It sneaks around and makes itself at home intending to take up permanent residence. I rip out rhizomes, shake roots free of soil and cram the basket full. My fingertips brush against stinging nettles left for butterflies to lay their eggs. My skin is nettle rashed and burning red as I dump the basket load in the chook yard. Through the chicken-wire mesh I watch the hens scratching, tossing scraps and chattering away with small talk.

The threat of frost eases. Soil is sun-warmed and rain-drenched. Days are balmy. Seeds sprout. Flowers unfold. Foamy blossoms explode in the orchard. The garden is alive with movement and sound. The air is thick with insects. Furred bees bumble about. Opening and closing their wings cabbage moths skip across broccoli. Dragonflies twirl gilded wings. Ladybirds, grasshoppers and spiders are snatched in flight by whirling fantails. From mud-brick nests, swallows dart down on quivery wings.

Picking lavish bunches of flowers seems an extravagance living so far off the beaten track. Early blooming annuals, larkspur spires, starry blurs of love-in-the-mist and sweet peas have an exciting quality. Mid-morning is a good time to gather a dew-fresh bouquet. Clouds are pencilled across blue sky. I snip into pea stems scrambling through the cross-stitched obelisks.

I prefer to grow species sweet peas. Although the traditional Spencer variety flowers are smaller and less flamboyant than the showier hybrids, their strength of scent is unmatched. The peas revel in the heat but prefer mulch-cool roots and limed soil. I gather bunches of sweet-smelling spikes and arrange them in the basket. Regular picking sets off blooms for weeks on end. When ripe pods crack open, I snap the seeds straight into a paper bag and store it in a rat-safe jar.

Inside, the peas fill a cream jug by the kitchen window. The downy leaves and curly tendrils set off the frilly flowers. Deeper crimson and purple tones balance the mauves and shell-pink shades. The scent wanders through the whole house.

The garden transforms. In soft sunlight, rosemary hedges glisten like wombat bristles. Grapevines bulge with buds of fur.

Summer

Sun and wind suck the garden dry. Water conservation is crucial with such free-draining soil. The bore supply is bottomless but we don't waste a drop. Water is a valuable resource we don't take for granted.

Our watering system is clumsy but water-wise. It's not high pressure. It's not set-and-forget. More string-round-the-finger remember. Taps are turned on and off. Hoses are dragged around by hand. Spiders clog sprinkler heads. Plastic pipe can leak, but it does the job. The pump chugs away, sucking water from the bore and driving it up to the tank. Tiny nozzle sprinklers fountain spray so fine that the water soaks gently and deeply without run-off, so there is less waste. Thornbills and wrens bathe. Silver eyes, robins and golden whistlers take a shower, fly through the spray, fluff out feathers, flick and splash in and out of the droplets.

Wind rubs the garden threadbare. It frays at the edges. More mulch stitches it together. The pitchfork jabs the odd sock, jocks and torn plastic bag as we pile pyramids of shredded waste collected from the tip. Mulch holds in moisture. It smothers weeds, cuts down evaporation and keeps the earth cool. It is as energy efficient as insulation bats or double-glazed windows. Mulch is a security blanket tossed over the garden. In unrelenting heat and shallow soil, for some plants mulching can mean the difference between life and death.

The vegetable garden is soaked. Deep, once-a-week watering encourages roots to wander off in search of reserves. Seedlings and leafy guzzlers are given priority. The bore water feels sulphurous on the skin. It's clean and mineral-rich, spattering leaves with salt crystals.

Salads are the mainstay of summer meals. Gathering greens for speedy salads and lazy lunches becomes a daily routine. Buttery mignonette, crisp iceberg, endive, mizuna, baby spinach, spicy nasturtium leaves for a bit of bite and whatever is available are washed of grit and slugs, drained in the colander, torn and jumbled together. Leaves are swirled with olive oil and a squeeze of lemon juice, tumbled with cherry tomatoes, garnished with garlic and basil. Radicchio's burgundy-red white-marbled rosettes, roma rosso, nutty sugarloaf, sharp, bitter, long-leaf chicory and peppery rocket complement the milder, non-hearting oak leaf lettuces. Whole radicchio is delicious brushed with olive oil and char-grilled on a hot griddle. Curved cucumbers are sliced and salted.

Tomatoes are mandatory in the summer garden. Heritage or heirloom tomatoes, time-capsule varieties selected from backyards and handed down through the generations for hundreds of years are renowned for their vigour and continual yields. Tomatoes crop from late December to May though seasons vary. Each summer we trial and taste test different varieties. Cherry, currant, pear and egg shapes, red, speckled, streaky, stripe-green and golden colours are ornamental but full flavours are the real drawcard. I have a soft spot for brandywine, beefsteak and the creamy-textured charcoal-fleshed black Russian. Mortgage lifter, bite-sized yellow-flecked tigrella and green zebra are all tasty varieties that have cropped well. I grow the old faithful Rouge de Marmande's knobbly fruit as a personal tradition. Trained marble-sized cherry tomatoes decorate the obelisks like balls on a culinary Christmas tree.

Trusses of sugar-bomb sweet Italian cherry tomato A Grappoli Da Inverno, full-gloss roma and skin-tight Principe Borghese are quartered, squeezed of seeds, salted and sun-dried on sheets of corrugated iron for five days (two to three for semi-dried) and brought in under cover at night. When late summer showers dampen our ideas we finish off drying in the stove overnight. The fruit is turned face down and dried until almost leathery but not crisp. Olive oil is poured over shrivelled tomatoes packed in bay leaves, garlic and sprinkled with oregano or basil. For seed collection we pick only good, fully over-ripened fruit from the bottom trusses.

Tomato Seed

Squash fruit by hand. Scoop out seeds. Stir in a jar of water to loosen seeds. Shake jar. Leave to ferment on a warm windowsill for a few days. Skim off scum. Strain and wash. Spread seeds on kitchen paper. Dry out. Store in an envelope in a cool dry place or in the fridge. In spring plant out paper in a tray of soaked potting mix and cover with compost.

Red currants shine with the lustre of rubies. As blackbirds slink off with most of the crop there is never enough for jelly. What can be salvaged is dusted with castor sugar and scattered over fresh fruit salad.

Raspberries for breakfast is bliss, if wallabies don't barge through a left-open gate, strip the canes and get caught red-handed. Crimson fruits hide among pleated leaves. Ripe berries shine as tempting as lip-sticked lips waiting to be kissed. Raspberries prefer acidic soil, shelter from raw winds and relish thick blankets of compost. We straw-mulch to keep the soil refrigerator-cool and sponge-moist through the dry weeks. The variety Nootka crops in spring and autumn. Williamette crops in spring and flushes in autumn. Both varieties need thorough soaking in this sandy soil to set fruit. Prickly canes are tenacious and know no bounds. Suckers take off in all directions and need ruthless control.

Walnut-sized shallots are wrapped in crackly coats. I braid the semi-green stems and hang the brassy bulbs to air-dry in the kitchen. Garlic loves the light soil. We grow two crops yearly, pressing cloves in limed compost in early May and October. Leaves and stems are twisted then bent over before digging. This stops the bulb from producing too much green. When the leaves brown off I pull fist-sized bulbs, rinse the root hairs, then braid withered stems to join ropes of shallots strung up to dry out of the sun. The knuckles are mild and crunchy when freshly dug in early summer and late autumn. Raffia-brittle skins wrinkle as garlic's nutty smell flavours summer nights.

Mother Nature gets busy with her housework. She polishes artichokes, buffs up waxy capsicums, burnishes black aubergines until they shine, ties beans with string, gift-wraps corncobs in paper-thin parcels, curls parsley hair and dresses leek seed heads in peaked pixie caps. She tidies up. Winds sweep paths and vacuum under beds. Seed pods empty. Summer showers rinse leaves.

We wake to the ping of rosellas. Magpies, whipbirds and wattlebirds mark their territories. Colours are fresh. Starburst potato flowers, coriander lace clouds and blue borage resemble an earth sky. Fantails, thornbills and silver eyes perform acrobatics on seeding fennel and parsnips. Fruit tree boughs are laden with rouge-cheeked peaches. Lemon verbena brushes my hand. I rub its citrus leaves into my fingers and sniff. Long-limbed sunflowers lure blue-shouldered rosellas to prise open seed heads and litter the ground with husks.

Mid-summer mornings in the vegetable garden are worth an early rise. Trapped sun warms still-damp earth. Water drops glisten like tears on the weeping leaves of sweet corn. Sea breeze fans the silk of unripe husks. Overnight, spiders have sewn webs. Dill seed heads shimmer in the patched light. Long shadows shorten as the sun shifts west. Lacewings and ladybirds zigzag. Pom-pom pink-mauve garlic and leek seed heads are bejewelled with ladybirds, beetles and bluebottles.

I always convince myself it's the gardener's privilege to graze for sun-still-on-them strawberries before the children or blackbirds make off with them. Scarlet, seed-speckled fruits are necklaced around collared leaves like chunky beads. I pinch off a berry and pop it in my mouth. It tastes sugary and buttery and cool on the tongue. I tear off a few purple king beans and a cucumber hidden behind the leaves' tendrils curled through the obelisk. Ribboned leaves rustle as I snap off cobs of corn. We chomp get-your-teeth-into-it sweet corn steamed with mint and butter for breakfast or char-grill in dampened husks.

Just a tickle of tomato leaves on my hand sets off the smell of childhood summers. Vine-ripened tomatoes are tasty but most are ripened out of the sun before harlequin bugs eat their way through them or blackbirds peck them to pieces. I snip two red and three turning-pink at the base, keeping the stalks intact. I carry the morning's harvest inside my hat for a breakfast of rye toast topped with tomato and basil and a pot of tea.

When late summer changes gear the potager goes off the rails. Road rules are out the window. Vegetables nudge one another and crowd out the neighbours. Plants run rag-tag, rushing ahead, disobeying orders to keep off footpaths.

It's peak hour all day. The warm air is traffic-jammed with butterflies, cabbage moths and horn-blaring bluebottles. Rhino beetles are revved-up and whizzing eye-high. Silver eyes stop over. Helicopter dragonflies take off or come in for landing. Marchflies touch down. Duco-black beetles beep. Bugs buzz bumper to bumper. Bees refuel. Bull ants ride the shuttle service. A convoy of ants accelerates foot-to-the-floor. Workers transport cargo: drag a moth carcass, pull a load of crumb or drop down a manhole. Road works in progress. Skinks scooter past. Blue-tongues stop-go. Snails move house. Slaters keep left, look right or give way. Crickets keep the ignition running. A blowie cadges a lift on the gardener's shoulder. A wattlebird screeches. The wheelbarrow blows a tyre and there's no spare. Asparagus fern runs to seed. Sunflower headlamps flick on high beam. Parsnip, fennel, dill and leek gone-to-seed, skyscraper up. Sprawling pumpkin vines jostle for space. In asphalt shadows, insects hover, waiting for the lights to change. Bats catch the night flight. And the slow-train sea rumbles.

When we go off-duty for a few days in summer I feel as if I am a captain jumping ship. Mulch is left as a plant survival kit. It is a lifebuoy equivalent thrown overboard to the whole garden. Can it stay afloat? Though the rest of the garden can fend for itself for a while, the vegie patch is saturated. Pots are soaked and are shoved into the shade where possible.

On our return I check out what the vegies have been up to. The garden's gone troppo. Left-alone gardens have a mind of their own. Crimp-edged squash resemble over-sized cupcakes baked too long in the oven. Little-finger cucumbers have swollen arm-thick. Capsicums have keeled over. Corn silks have shrivelled. Swollen husks are ready to be guzzled. Rats have bitten some cobs clean. A tide of tomatoes is screaming to be picked. Vine leaves grovel along the ground. Lettuces are limp. Basil has wilted. Spinach seedlings have snuffed it. Midget beans have shot up to giants. Weeds have snuck in while no one was looking. A wombat has been up to no good. Slugs have polished off the parsley. The plum tree has dropped its bird-pecked fruit. Rabbit-chomped cabbages rear their ugly heads. Misshapen zucchinis are double-chinned and bordering on obesity. Pumpkins are throwing their weight around. Droopy, tubbed lemon trees bounce back after a squirt with a kinking hose.

Zucchini parachutes make a joyful welcome home dish. We open out the petals, shake off any insects, cut out stamens, stuff with a mixture of rice, fetta and thyme, twist the ends and steam whole. The flowers cook quickly and their flavour is hit-the-spot sweet ; great finger-food dipped in batter and fried. Fresh and firm, morning-open flowers need to be gathered daily before they swell to fruits.

Deep-Fried Zucchini Flowers

2 eggs
20 zucchini flowers
150 grams flour
olive oil
salt and pepper

Whisk seasoned eggs with a fork. Dip flowers in egg mix. Dust with flour. Drop into hot oil until crispy. Drain. Serve with sea salt, pepper and wedges of lemon.

On the verandah shaded by twisty grapevines, we slump into cane chairs crusted with bird droppings. We knock the top off a bottle of beer. The light fades. Slug trails glitter silver across the bricks. Doors are flung open. A sea breeze wafts through flywire windows. Orange tiger lilies light up a black vase. Lazy summer sounds fill the night. The sprinkler splutters, damping down pumpkin vines. Splashings spit as high as the fence tops. Descending twilight smells of musk, vanilla, bursaria and fermenting fruit.

Autumn

Summer's spent crops are hauled away. In two of the three bins Terry bashed together from sheets of corrugated iron a visitor donated, garden trash, weeds, eggshells, tea-leaves, seaweed, chicken and sheep manure are dumped and spread slapdash in alternating layers. Sprinkling blood and bone, scattering shovelfuls of wood ash from the fire and stove and chucking on handfuls of comfrey do the trick of stirring in some life and triggering off decay. Wrapped in a straw blanket, the pile will home brew all winter and collapse to rum-coloured loam. It's rags to riches when what has been taken from the earth will be put back.

I usually trickle out broad bean seeds in April. Broadies are prone to rust here if planted too early. I bend, kneel and drag the rake across the bed, sowing bok choy, mizuna and slow-bolting cut-and-come-again oriental vegetable seeds. Silver beet and mustard spinach sow their own seeds for on-going greens. Parsnips self-seed in the same bed for years.

On cloudy post-rain days, I tuck seedlings in to strawy nests. I dote on youngsters for the first week or two, offering sips of water and seaweed liquid lunches. They are then expected to get by without spoon-feeding. Welsh bunching onion clumps are split and poked in around beds. Shooting cloves of golden shallots and leek bulbils are pressed into the soil and limed.

The air is blizzard-thick with cabbage moths. Torn ears of blue-veined cabbages, broccoli and brussels sprouts poke out when the moths leave. Artichoke stalks are chopped off with a sharp-edged shovel and spread as mulch. Plants are hacked in half, divided and dibbled into holes collared with compost. (They forgive me if I only get around to separating them every two or three years.)

Rhubarb clumps are long lived. Well-fed plants tuck in to hefty helpings of keep-your-strength-up compost and still ask for seconds. Rhubarb rewards us with crumpled, heart-shaped leaves and ruby stalks that can be pulled most of the year. Though summer stalks are thicker, rhubarb can be cooked in any season. We combine it with summer's white-fleshed nectarines and autumn's Granny Smith apples.

Crunchy Rhubarb Crumble

Chop up a good bunch of rhubarb stalks into chunks. Generously sprinkle on brown sugar. Simmer until soft (or over-cook till gooey) in a couple of tablespoons of water.

Rub 50 grams of softened butter into 100 grams of sugar and 150 grams of plain flour until crumbly. Flour can be substituted with ground almonds. Spread over fruit. Bake in an ovenproof dish at 180°C for 30-40 minutes until golden or juice bubbles through the crust. Sprinkle with dry-fry toasted almonds. Serve with fresh strawberries, a blob of whipped cream or scoops of ice-cream.

Rain pumps up the passionfruit. The fruits hang out in

purple-black leather jackets dotted across the chook-pen vine. Heavies plummet to the ground. I gather an armful of sun-wrinkled fruits, split a shrivelled hull and suck the warm pulp studded with seeds. Breakfast of yogurt, smothered in tahini and honey and squirted with passionfruit is a taste sensation.

We suffer a glut of tomatoes. We stagger with buckled knees, hauling baskets and bowls stuffed with egg tomatoes, cherry tomatoes and beefy black tomatoes as big as buns. Early morning, we snatch shirtfuls, skirtfuls and bulging string bagfuls. Tomatoes burst from buckets and boxes. They topple off washtubs stacked high on the hearth. Mounds of tomatoes sit dimpled and scarred, lumpy and leaking. Blemished and blotched, split and squashed, over-ripe and rotten, tomatoes roll round the kitchen floor. In the sink, I scrub off slaters and earwigs crawling out of cracks. I scour, skin, seed, slice and dice tomatoes to be grilled, slow-roasted, fried, dried and stewed.

The kitchen is a sea of sauces and soups, purees and pastes bubbling and spluttering in cast iron pots. Bench tops are puddled with bloody juice, pulpy pink flesh, curled skins and sticky seeds. The table is cluttered with preserving jars, lids, ladle, colander, strainer, knives and chopping boards stained red. I cackle with joy hunched over the stove, a witch boiling blood, stirring and slurping tastes from the wooden spoon. The perfume of tomatoes and garlic, basil, bay leaf and thyme wafts through the whole house.

When tomatoes tumble off the bench tops this recipe for home-made sauce eases the surplus.

Home-Made Tomato Sauce

1 tablespoon olive oil
2 cloves garlic, crushed

2 kilos tomatoes, skinned and chopped
1 tablespoon sugar
sprig rosemary or thyme
handful of torn basil leaves

Heat oil. Fry garlic. Add remaining ingredients. Season with sea salt and cracked black pepper Stir occasionally until sauce thickens.

This lasagne recipe varies with whatever is available in the garden. Zucchinis can be substituted with slices of char-grilled eggplant. Mushrooms can be added.

Vegetable Lasagne

packet pasta sheets or home-made
home-made tomato sauce
a few fresh tomatoes, chopped
bunch of spinach or silver beet cooked in salted water
2 zucchinis, sliced
One or two red capsicums, sliced (optional)
2 cloves garlic, chopped
mozzarella or sliced balls of bocconcini cheese (or leave out for a fat-
    free dish)
olive oil
salt and pepper

Arrange a layer of pasta sheets, then layers of sauce, tomatoes, spinach, zucchini, capsicum, garlic and cheese, sprinkling salt and pepper and drizzling olive oil as you go. Bake in hot oven (200°C). Home-made pasta sheets cook crispy on top. Cut into generous squares and serve with crusty bread to blot up sauce. Feeds four.

Stuffed tomatoes make a great entree. Serve hot or cold when peckish.

Stuffed Tomatoes

8 large tomatoes
8 anchovies, chopped
handful pipped black olives (kalamata)
1-2 cloves garlic, chopped
spring onion, chives or parsley, chopped
50 grams breadcrumbs
cracked black pepper

Cut tops off tomatoes. Scoop out flesh. Mix ingredients together. Stuff mixture into hollowed-out tomatoes. Sprinkle with extra breadcrumbs. Bake in hot oven (200°C) for about 20 minutes without lids until crumbs are crispy. Serve with lids and a glass of wine. Buon appetito.

Winter

Winter stands idle in grey gaberdine. Coat-tails flap as it turns up its collar and gives me the cold shoulder. The days move at hearse pace. The potager is a cemetery of weeds. The compost heap's a pile of corpses. Obelisks echo war monuments hung with dead flower wreaths, weeks after the memorial service.

Frosted artichoke leaves seem sugar coated. Mountains of mulch seem snow-capped. Beach sands are brushed white and crusted right down to Anderson's Inlet. Snapping ice thaws. Leaves sparkle in the weak sunshine.

Low-angled sun casts long shadows. Plants are lit from the side. Days get shorter. Winter is a skinflint. The garden lives in poverty, hoarding nutrients.

Some days I am reluctant to leave the kitchen comfort zone. But the plan to bake a vegie pie fuels the need to duck out for the ingredients. I shawl a jumper over my shoulders, grab the basket, carving knife and scissors and make a bolt for the blustery world outside, ready to ransack. Four and twenty blackbirds sneak into shadows, skulk along paths or fly off when they spot me.

A heavy-handed wind slaps me on the face and brings me to my senses. I had forgotten winter's economical landscape and chalky light. In the draughty garden rooms, my eyes scan for signs of life. Mustard spinach's crinkled green and burgundy leaves would seem a non-event in any other season. Pale jonquils brave the cold. Early morning frost has stiffened weeds. Limited colour and shapes heighten sounds. A shrike thrush sings a note. Though scents are dulled, white-lipped, black-eyed broad bean flowers flutter their perfume.

Desiccated clouds fringe the sky. Frost streaks shimmer in sunlight. Beds are hushed with mulch. Currant twigs and hazelnuts hung with catkins reveal their naked beauty. Pyramid obelisks spear the sky. Bony ribs stick out. Spring seems as far away as distant Egypt. But tombs hold treasure. Seeds hatch from the casings of burial chambers. Snow pea tendrils tickle the obelisks' legs. Summer's purple and streaky-gold beans will dangle jewellery fit for a pharaoh.

My knife decapitates a savoy cabbage. It topples over. The crumpled skirt and brocaded petticoats almost fill the basket. I slash a cross through the stump for baby cabbages to sprout on each quarter. Sharp winds can shred cabbages to coleslaw. Caterpillars can gnaw leaves to lace. I flick off a slug and, staining my fingers, squash two caterpillars. The chill improves curly kale's strong flavour, but its blue leaves are so decorative it escapes the knife. Curled cauliflowers are still forming, cocooned like pearls, protected by cradling leaf arms.

Root crops are valiant vegetables and reliable winter foods. Carrots and nutty parsnips taste even better lifted in cold weather. I wrench a hand of fat-fingered carrots and leave a patch for summer's lace-white flowers. These stumpy carrots are crunchy, sweet and juicy when pulled fresh. Fern tops will be sprinkled as a garnish. A yellow-breasted robin darts into the soil to snatch an insect. Creamy parsnip shoulders are showing. I snap off stalks of crinkled chard. The springy leaves are bulky in the basket. I slice through leeks just below the shaft so they will re-shoot and pinch out a handful of broad bean leaf tips. My scissors snip a posy of rabbit-bitten parsley, a few chives and toss them in the basket.

I wade knee-deep through weeds, trudge along the unswept paths and head for the house. Threads of smoke weave their way from the chimney. Sunlight segments the kitchen. The room is welcoming. The kettle throbs. I stoke the fire, squat and press my back into the warmth of the oven door. The stove is the heart of the house. It's where the family gathers in the morning. It heats the water, cooks our food, dries winter washing and keeps the cuppas coming. Boots warp on the slate hearth. Steaming socks hang on the towel rail. My cold hands cup hot tea as I thaw out and sniff in the smells of damp leather and wet trousers.

The oven is the core of our winter cooking. I scrub the vegetables under a running tap in the laundry wash-trough, rinsing out grit, slugs, earwigs and tiny spiders. Clean vegetables are heaped on the marble bench top ready to be topped and tailed. In the light spilling down from the skylight the wet vegetables shine.

There is so much pleasure from picking, preparing and eating seasonal foods. If it's raining, I often spend mornings mucking around in the kitchen, staring out the window, making up recipes, chopping up vegetables for slow-cooked soups, roasting sweet-fleshed pumpkin and potatoes, coring and peeling apples to put together a home-style fruit crumble or crusted pie. The steamy smells and heart-warming flavours keep out the cold. This made-up recipe for baked butternuts is simple but sumptuous.

Baked Butternut Pumpkin

Cut small pumpkins in half lengthways. Scoop out seeds. Mix a couple of finely chopped tomatoes, torn basil leaves, a clove of minced garlic, fresh chopped chilli or paste to taste, salt and lots of black pepper. Stuff mixture into hollows. Shave on parmesan cheese or drizzle on olive oil and bake in a hot oven (200°C) for about 40 minutes or until soft and golden. Serve in skin. One pumpkin half per person.

ORCHARD

A blood plum tree dominated my family's backyard. In spring my fingers brushed its leafy tufts. The tree was in blossom on my birthday in September. Soon after, it broke out in green bumps. It seemed forever till the branches blushed with rosy-cheeked fruits. The smell scented summer nights when my brother and I sat on the woodshed roof slurping the wine-coloured juice. We sucked the life from those blood plums with the relish of vampires. We spat out the pips and flicked them on to the roof of next door's toilet. Wherever we went we left a trail of plum stones behind us.

In broad daylight our gang thieved loquats and cherry plums from overhanging branches. Prized apricots and harder-to-come-by nectarines were nicked at night. We took turns bunking each other up onto one another's shoulders to shake the out-of-reach branches where all the best fruit seemed to be. Daredevils climbed laneway fences and peeked into kitchen windows, secretly hoping to be chased by a trouser-tearing dog or fist-shaking tree owner. Heroes came out bragging cut hands. We smuggled the contraband in a jumper and headed back to the hideout where with wet-your-pants excitement we scoffed the lot. Though forbidden fruit tastes sweeter, I always knew one day I would grow my own.

Orchards are steeped in horticultural history. The Persians treasured them as sacred places of pleasure and beauty, but the origins of our orchard were far from romantic.

Twiggy trees held high hopes. We had visions of a fruit forest but tragedy struck. Buds and leaves that sprouted over weeks were munched in minutes. Through sheer ignorance we planted the trees unfenced. Nobody warned us. Kangaroos love fruit trees.

We caged the trees in chicken-wire. Thin-armed saplings scratched at the sky. When the much-needed fence was finally finished the smell of sump oil and creosote slapped on the palings was better than any perfume.

But a fence wasn't enough. Apricots struggled to bear fruit. Rabbits ring-barked the trunks. It was the orchard's first brush with death. Other let-downs followed. Our time with cherries was short and sweet. The weakened trees were doomed from the start and couldn't go the distance. The failed crop of a handful of fruit was our last. Even seasons later when we caught on that olives would do well here, one tree gave up in its second summer. We learned the hard way that in sandy soil, deep watering and heavy mulching are crucial for the survival of young trees.

Years down the track the orchard pulls its weight through the seasons. Blossoms flood spring's branches for summer's peaches, plums and nectarines. Autumn's apples, nashis, pears, figs and quince flavours extend through winter in fruit pies, preserves and jams. Winter trees' frames show off brindled barks. Cropping is spasmodic. It's feast or famine as some boughs bend with fruit one year and bear nothing the next.

As most of the garden's trees are evergreen, there are only a few autumn flutterings from the deciduous fruit trees. The space-saving pair of nashis espaliered against the picket fence are streaked with buttery leaves to match the fruit's matt-gold skin. The trees open long arms in May, stripping down to a bare beauty. Apple and pear trees have a more belated modesty and don't undress until well into winter when branches and calloused fingers show their age.

Long-handled loppers perform surgery in winter. Peach, nectarine, apple and pear trees' overlapping branches are amputated. Plums are left alone apart from cutting out any dead limbs. I scalpel my way through pruning now the trees are shaped.

Growing vegetables between the trees uses space, mulch and water more efficiently. It only works because the vegetables grown are no-dig-easy-pick, so tree roots are not disturbed. Potatoes produce maximum results for minimum effort. In spring I gamble with frosts playing Russian roulette rolling out seed potatoes like dice, smothering with compost and blankets of warm straw. If the sun shows its hand and frost-free luck comes up trumps, small spuds crop before Christmas. It's double or nothing. Loser or winner. When haulms yellow I burrow in to hit jackpots of waxy, yellow-fleshed patrones and pink fir apple potatoes. Baby spuds, steamed whole, unpeeled, rolled in melted butter, salted and sprinkled with chopped chives, parsley and lovage, melt in the mouth. Pink-skinned desirees are perfect for potato salad, garlic-herbed gnocchi or roasted brushed with olive oil and sprinkled with salt and rosemary.

Fat-bellied pumpkins bully their way between the potatoes.

In mid-spring seeds are pressed into mounds of one wheelbarrow load each of manure, compost and mulch. Bohemian chestnut, blue hubbard's warty fruits, bell-shaped butternuts and grapefruit-sized orange-skinned golden nugget are all tasty pumpkins we still grow, narrowed down from a once-wider range. By early summer, runners rub against late Flanders poppies and scramble over the retaining walls, carpeting a living mulch beneath the trees.

Summer's juice-spurting peaches are slurped straight from the tree. We pick over windfall fruit and toss jam-sticky nectarines into a cardboard box. The pointy, purple-black, yellow-fleshed plum Prune D'Agen has never cropped heavily. In a good season only a hatful of fruit is dried whole in the shade or pitted, flattened and sun-cured. The rich-flavoured plums shrivel to chewy treats that can be stuffed with marzipan, or stored.

Summer's odours saturate the orchard. The sickly sweet stench of bruised peaches and what's left of the nectarines stew in the high temperatures. Sun-caramelised onions, rotting seaweed, chicken manure, the stink of crushed ants and shrunken milk thistles sour in the sun. Summer is decomposing.

Flocks of silver eyes dressed in grey-breasted olive green suits and striking white eye rings, drop by for afternoon tea. Tiny beaks pierce heath berries, remaining red currants, plums and early grapes. The singsong of yellow-faced honeyeaters rings through the orchard. The birds raid whatever-they-can-get-away-with peaches and nectarines but provide a free service of pecking off grubs and aphids and usually leave enough fruit for everyone. Very obliging.

The orchard peaks in autumn. We pig-out on pears, guts

grapes and feed our faces with figs. Quinces' furred fruits glow luminous yellow. The fruit scent is a cross somewhere between apples, pears and lemons. The tree is worth a place for its pale pink flower and fuzzy-bottom leaves alone. Quinces prefer moist drained soil but seem to be adaptable. Our single tree's fruit fills a packing case though the hangers-on are usually parrot-pecked.

The quince was esteemed in ancient Greece and Persia. Today it is often snubbed as a second-rate citizen and considered riff-raff in the fruit world. But in my family its tart taste has always held legendary status. My cousins and I pursed our lips whenever we bit into the grainy raw flesh. Every autumn, my grandmother Vera hauled in a wash tub full of fruit from her backyard tree. She transformed the strained, bulky pulp into a transparent crimson-pink quince jelly. Its perfume filled the kitchen. I have adapted her half-remembered, half-pinched recipe (thanks Stephanie) to carry on the tradition. It's fiddly but worth the trouble.

Nanna's Quince Jelly

Pick fifteen to twenty quinces when fragrant and turning green-yellow. More mature, deeper gold-yellow fruit contains less pectin and is unsuited to making jelly. Riper fruit is better baked or slow-poached in honey.

Wash and chop half of the fruit into chunks. The skin, pips and core contain pectin and are not removed. Chop-and-drop into a bowl of water to which a squeeze of lemon has been added so fruit keeps its colour. Cover with water in a saucepan and slowly simmer to a pulp. Strain liquid. Discard pulp. Chop remaining fruit and slow-cook in quince liquid for about an hour. Scald cheesecloth with boiling water so liquid flows freely though it. Pour fruit through cloth-lined colander. Resist the temptation to press down, as this will make the liquid cloudy. Allow to drip overnight. Discard fruit. To every 500ml of strained liquid add 400 grams of sugar. Bring to boil for 15 minutes. Skim off foam. When cool, sprinkle with a few drops of rosewater (optional). Ladle into jars and seal.

Granny Smiths, Gravensteins, Red Delicious, Jonathans, espaliered Pink Lady and the eighteenth-century heritage Cox's Orange Pippin combined ensure a supply of crisp, squeaky-skinned, sticker-free eating apples for pies and crumbles. Granny Smith sweetens if ripened on the tree. Pippins picked before ripening develop a mellow flavour. The organically grown apples are often smaller than shop bought and the fruit is sometimes more blemished than commercial crops, but good looks and flavour don't always go hand in hand.

We soon stumbled across the orchard's shy next-door neighbours tucked away in the bush minding their own business. It was as if we had uncovered an out-of-place semi-tropical Garden of Eden. Five feral fig trees spread tangled branches and wide-fingered, open-palmed leaves like welcoming arms. The fig tree, indigenous to Persia and Syria, symbol of peace and plenty, is one of the most ancient plants in civilisation.

Fig trees are a miracle. Ours self-sustain on starved sand and neglect. Summer's green nipples develop to breast-shaped fruit. As leaves curl and yellow, we jump up, bend down branches and tear off stems dripping with milky sap that burns too-greedy lips. Over-ripe figs are sun-warm and weighty, swollen and stick-in-the-teeth sweet. Purple-brown skinned figs burst open to magenta flesh. Waves of silver eyes squeak through the branches pecking out the fruit until the skins hang like lanterns. Figs ripen a few at a time so are picked day-to-day to get in quick.

Late figs are sun and wind dried on wire racks. This takes a few days. Dry figs keep well pressed into blocks and stored in an airtight container. We mix the shrunken fruits with hazelnuts and chocolate in my sister Julie's recipe for an Italian-style fig torta. It's easy to make and contains no added sugar, relying on the fruit and chocolate for sweetness.

Fig Torta

250 g roasted hazelnuts
250 g roasted almonds
250 g dried figs
$1/2$ cup mixed peel
250 g dark cooking chocolate
3 eggs
1 $1/4$ cups self-raising flour
juice of an orange or lemon, or grated lemon rind

Mix roughly chopped nuts, fruit, peel and chocolate together. Beat eggs and add to fruit mix. Gradually add in sifted flour. Squeeze in juice. Pour mixture into greased tin and cook in a moderate oven (180° C) for about an hour. A treat served with coffee.

We brush figs with olive oil and grill. We bake figs splashed in Grand Marnier. We marinate halved figs in brandy or cointreau with a shake of sugar, sprinkle with a few fresh raspberries and top-off with whisked cream or dollops of mascarpone and grated chocolate.

The larder is stocked ceiling-high with fig and ginger jam. I bought jars of this jam at my children's school Easter Fair. I took a stab at the recipe but could never get it right. I finally tracked down Heather, its maker, and extracted the recipe.

Heather's Fig and Ginger Jam

3 kilos ripe fresh figs
2 kilos sugar
1 cup vinegar
$^1/_2$ cup lemon juice
generous hand of freshly grated ginger
4 tablespoons lemon rind

Chop figs into large chunks or quarters. Place in a ceramic bowl. Cover with sugar. Leave to stand overnight. Transfer to a pan. Add vinegar, juice, ginger and lemon rind. Boil 30-40 minutes until set. When cool pour into sterilised jars and seal.

Bees reside in a run-down high-rise apartment hive under an apple tree. The tenants mysteriously moved house with no forwarding address then moved back a couple of years later. Most of the time we leave them alone. On occasion bee-keeper Terry has robbed the hives and extracted wax-crusted frames. We gorge chunks of honeycomb, lick drippy fingers and chew beeswax. Late spring's pale honey captures the dense flavour of tea-tree blossom in a jar. Summer-autumn's honey is treacle-sticky. Its golden-syrup colour, fudgy texture and smoky flavour reek of banksia nectar.

A hedge of fifty hazelnuts borders the orchard and vegetable garden. Hazelnut trees stretch to two metres. Spring's branches dangle pollen-dusted catkins. Summer scorches crinkled leaves. Hazelnuts are shallow-rooted and need moisture, thick layers of mulch, compost and a kick along with blood and bone to crop in the sandy soil. Only a few of the cross-pollinating varieties American White and Cosford began to bear nuts after about seven years. Shade-stunted trees have struggled to stay alive.

By late autumn, hazelnut clusters fall to the ground. Remaining leaves shrivel parchment-stiff. Faded yellow husks tinged pink-brown and curled at the edges fit like pillowslips around the nuts rattling in pointed wooden shells. Before any chance of mould, we gather them up, snap the stems, peel off the papery husks and drop them in a sack. The nuts are spread out on sheets of newspaper to dry on the kitchen floor for a few days then stored in the rat-proof cellar of the cottage. Through winter we black-roast hazelnuts and smash the shells by the fire. The skins crackle and shatter to dust.

A hedge of twenty feijoa trees, or pineapple guavas, adjoins the orchard at the garden entrance. Ripe autumn fruits drop like manna from heaven. Pale green suede bags hold a tropical pineapple-strawberry flavour. Feijoas are frost-hardy and don't seem fussy about soil. The trees were summer-watered for the first couple of years but as adolescents they get by with heavy mulching alone. Summer's red-stamened flowers are similar to a eucalypt blossom.

The established fruit trees need less attention. Compost and mulch are the only form of feeding (apart from a pet cemetery of dead chooks, ducks, rabbits and guinea pigs buried beneath the trees). The heavy bearers are figs, pears, apples, peaches and nectarines. We snatch what we can before blackbirds, rosellas and wattlebirds help themselves to what they think is their fair share of the profits.

We find pears taste zestier if ripened off the tree. Picking the fruit unripened also cuts down wind damage and beats the birds. Gold-yellow espaliered Kosui and Twentieth Century nashis resemble small apples. Ripe fruit is picked when crisp, sweet and juicy. Cinnamon-skinned, long-necked Beurre Boscs are usually ready before the big and bumpy Packhams. The pears are delicious poached in red wine.

Frost chills autumn mornings. It blisters the fruit trees' fingers and sends a shiver down the orchard's spine. Pumpkin leaves blacken with rot. Gourds rattle with seeds. Tomato vine stalks melt to mush. Pumpkins cling to vines until the stems waste away. Butternuts last for months if stored in a cool, dry place. Matured seeds are scooped out a few weeks after picking, stuffed in labelled envelopes, pegged on the line to dry further for a day and then stored in a screw-top jar.

Unpicked fruits hang like memos to harvest. Quinces plop to the ground. Apples bounce down the stone steps and roll into weeds smelling of juice fermenting .

Shrinking passionfruit cling to loose-leaf vines. Grapes lap up the sun and poor soil. Tendrils strangle wrist-thick vines shading the chook yard all summer. Veined leaves are as broad as a man's hand. We do nothing but prune and mulch with stone rubble.

Table grapes Waltham Cross and raisin-dark black muscats hang in clusters. Ripe grapes are now netted or tied in individual bunches in brown paper bags before they can be sucked dry by silver eyes or pecked off by wattlebirds. We snip off bunches with scissors. The grapes are sun-sweet, thick-skinned and crunchy with seeds. Young vine leaves are plunged into salted boiling water, pickled with a squeeze of lemon juice and served as wrappers for stuffed parcels of rice, crumbled fetta, garlic and thyme.

Grapevines are clothed in claret-purple bunches. The sun squeezes out grape juice. It presses cider from apples. Handfuls of olives shine wine-red and ripen to black. Winter chill helps to set Manzanillo's fruits. We jiggle the branches or whack with a stick, and olives rattle onto the tarp, ready for pickling.

The fragrance of rotting quinces drifts through the orchard. I prop the stepladder against the pear-tree trunk and climb. The bird's-eye view changes scale and perspective. Garden beds below shrink. The surf hums louder. Banksia treetops flame rose pink in the late afternoon light. Pears glimmer like party-light bulbs against the greying sky. The tree is loaded. I shake the spurred top branches and pears shoot down like bullets. Some are as big as bombs and crash-land with a thud. We peel the Packhams when silky and slippery and the juice is at dribbling point. When the flesh is firm and crunchy we chomp into them skin-and-all.

My hitched-up skirt bulges with a few pears and lumpy tomatoes banging against my thighs. Brittle leaves crackle under my boots as I stagger inside to turn the fruit into pickles and chutney.

My gardener-cook buddy Annie sent me this recipe to use up the season's late tomatoes. Works every time.

Ripe Tomato Relish

3 kilos ripe skinned tomatoes, roughly chopped

2 kilos Granny Smith apples, peeled, cored and sliced

1 kilo brown sugar

50 grams sultanas (optional)

3 large onions, sliced

5 cloves chopped garlic

500 mls white wine vinegar

1 tablespoon salt

1 tablespoon ground cinnamon

1 tablespoon dry mustard

1 tablespoon ground ginger

1 teaspoon cayenne pepper

Combine all ingredients in a large pan. Stir over heat until sugar is dissolved. Let it bubble away. Keep an eye on it and give it a stir. Simmer for about two to three hours or until thick. Allow to cool. Ladle into jars and seal.

COTTAGE GARDEN

Cottage gardens enchant me. When I was seven I used to spy on my neighbour, Mrs Wilson, pottering in her front garden. I pressed my cheek against the side fence palings and peeked. Daubs of colour mingled to make a charming picture window.

The framed illustration came to life. Pelargonium, daisies, phlox, candytuft and mignonette hid the path winding from the gate to her front door. Her cobweb hair glistened as she chipped away with the hoe. We became mates and I wandered the paths, popping fuchsia buds, wriggling my tongue into honeysuckle and rattling a stick along the front fence hedged with wormwood. Its bitter smell still triggers my memory of Mrs Wilson.

When I was eight I built my first garden by the briquette shed. Honey-coloured rocks bordered a semi-circular bed. Dad bought me a playing-card sized packet of marigold seeds. In my palm the black lines resembled brush bristles dipped in white paint. I crouched down and dragged my finger through the soil crumbs to form a groove. I scattered the seeds, brushed my fingertips across the earth and patted it down. The watering can trickled a shower. The soil darkened. Green specks poked through only days after planting. It was magic. Weeks later marigolds glowed in citrus shades of lemon and tangerine against the tawny rocks and pitch-black coal dust. It imprinted an indelible picture in my mind. My grown-up garden is just a bigger version.

Early cottage gardens were established as utilitarian food gardens. After the orchard and vegetable garden were up and running, this one began with some cabbages and a few flowers. There was no sketching out ideas. No pen to paper. No master plan. If there was even a peep of what could be called a vision, it was short sighted. Plant selection and associations, foliage and form were not even vaguely considered.

I was a sucker for street stalls. Girl Guides, Brownies and Boy Scouts. I sussed out markets, garage sales, garden clubs, church bazaars and country flower shows. I stalked Apex, Rotary and Lions Club caravans. I staked out school fetes and fairs. I tracked down charity fund-raisers: the Country Fire Authority and the Country Women's Association and Red Cross. My skin broke out in goosebumps at the sight of trestle tables loaded with humble herbs, puny geraniums and root-bound mints. Trays of just-hatched seedlings and plants well past it. Cuttings poked into cut-off cartons, halved milk containers, rusty jam tins, ice-cream buckets, hole-punched and dented kerosene tins. Daggy dahlias and dorky daisies. Crude and common. Half-grown and homey. Labelled with cardboard strips, icy-pole sticks or pencilled onto tin tags. Some remained nameless. Women In Aprons (WIA), Mothers' Clubs and Ladies' Auxiliaries sold them as 'shrubby something-or-other', 'tall thingumabob' or 'a wooly watchamacallit'. Backyard bits-and-pieces that wouldn't be caught dead in a designer garden.

Hidden among cream sponges in a cut-down cardboard box, jars of jam and knitted tea-cosies, a get-in-early gem would catch my eye. A succulent for fifty cents. Dill for a dollar. A nerine for next-to-nothing. Giveaway gladdies. An old-fashioned rose at two bucks a pop. Oddballs you'd never come across in a nursery. All at cheapskate prices. I bought up big and headed home with a boot full of polystyrene boxes squeaking with small gardens.

Ignorance was bliss. I planted on impulse. The sweet disorder of squeezed-in snapdragons, the haphazard jumble of zinnias and plonked-in pansies and whatever took my fancy were thrill enough. It was a naive freckling of flowers. Colours clashed. I was blind to scale, proportion and contrasts of dark and light. It was quaint but kitsch.

I mail ordered. I thumbed through catalogues. I ticked the gotta-gets and can't-live-withouts, circled the not-exactly-sures and question-marked the never-heard-ofs. I asterisked the wished-fors. I sent away for postage-stamp small and envelope-large plants, not considering climate, cost or conditions. Rare tulips from Tasmania? Dianthus dispatched from the Dandenongs? Magnolias mailed from Macedon? No Probs. A wave of the chequebook and parcels arrived by post. I ripped open brown paper wrapping on sticky-taped surprise packages marked, 'Beware Live Plants'. The kitchen table was piled with shredded magazines and scrunched up, still-damp newspapers. Styrene pellets, straw and sawdust were scattered across the top. Tucked between the bubble wrap and plastic wrap, bare-rooted or plastic-potted, rubber-banded and lovingly packed were the you-asked-for-its, sometimes complete with advice: 'Pop the bulbs in the crisper a few weeks before planting' and cheery hand-written messages from the grower: 'Enjoy. Drop in if you're down this way.' We planted out late autumn. Winter was wait-and-see. Spring delivered some flowers courier-quick. But by late summer most of the new arrivals were sun-damaged.

It got worse. The first summer garden was a dead loss. My attraction to woodland plants was fatal. I pandered to their every whim. Hellebores hung on by the skin of their teeth. Viburnums bit the dust. Hydrangeas had one foot in the grave. Leaves curled up like toes. Fritillarias awaited a near-death experience. Trilliums opted for voluntary euthanasia.

Summer was heartless. It turned its back on the exhausted, the needy and a blind eye to the dying. It sucked bone marrow from tender plants. Campanulas cried out for a drink. Delphiniums died without dignity. Species geraniums lay bone-stiff. Anemones made suicide pacts. Fuchsias withered away on their deathbeds. The body count rose daily. Some could not be identified.

I felt more like a mortician than a gardener. The wheelbarrow-stretcher-ambulance-coffin-with-the-lid-open-cart rattled as I wheeled out the deceased to the crematorium or buried them in shallow mass graves. Daisies were the only flowers this garden was pushing up. The post-mortem concluded: wrong plant wrong place.

My heart hardened. I became ruthless and abandoned plants in their hour of need. I stopped the daily diagnosis, the check-ups, doing the ward rounds as hospice nurse, bending ear-to-the-ground for a heart murmur, intensive-caring for casualties and terminally ill and bandaging the sick and suffering to stakes. I tore off the bandages, threw away the crutches, reduced visiting hours and cut off medication. I pulled the plug on life-support, took plants off the drip and ditched water-dependent perennials.

I had made bad choices. I was a junkie with a hang-the-expense habit. I had overdosed on flashy 'just-releaseds' in hot-pink pots with in-your-face labels and over-the-top price tags. I was hanging out with the wrong garden-centre crowd.

I finally took the hint from the surrounding bush. It took a while to click but the clues stared me in the face. Grey-green and silver plants. Tough leaves. I went into rehab. Got a hit from home grown. I made do with the stand-bys, propagating more-of-the-same that worked rather than those that dressed to impress. I scored only hard-nosed plants that could get through the day without an overdose of water.

The importance of preserving the integrity of the surrounds hit home. We began integrating the garden with the bush. Preference for silver-grey foliaged plants from similar climates has been part of the secret of success. Arid-area yuccas, succulents and Mediterranean lavender, rosemary and bay suit this coastal climate. Grouping gritty die-hards has curtailed feeding and watering. The 'Dos' and 'Don'ts' became clear but they were hard won by guesswork and heartbreaking trial and error.

Pining for paeonies? Hankering for hostas? Get over it. Forget 'What's In' and 'What's Out', ' What's Hot' and 'What's Not'. Forget pin-up plants. My top-of-the-pops are plants with attitude. Gutsy summer-long performers that grow in undernourished soil and survive on natural rainfall are the garden's greatest hits.

We avoided Coastal Weeds Most Wanted. Acanthus and crocosmia work in cahoots as escapee partners-in-crime. Plants selected would be inside jobs. Verbascum grew too well. Potential break-and-enter weeds or 'the ones that got away' placed them under investigation with sweet pittosporum, *Pittosporum undulatum,* and other outlaws at large or on the usual suspects list.

The grey-green garden reflects the bush. It's less self-conscious. It fits in. It gets on with the over-the-fence neighbours. The plants aren't dead ringers for the locals but they bear a resemblance. They may be a pale imitation but they come close. Though permanent residents and outsiders keep their distance, it's not 'us' and 'them' but more an arranged mixed marriage that works. Not-so-strange bedfellows living side by side. The silvers weld together. The match is not perfect, the joins are not seamless but the gap has been narrowed and the lines are blurred.

The plants grown are nothing special. The bottom-of-the-heap, run-of-the-mill selection would not excite name-droppers of rare varieties. Every plant has to earn its place and there are limited places here for the faint-hearted. It is survival of the fittest. Summer sorts out the workers from the wimps. In killer drought and knock-em-down winds they are the last ones standing.

But appropriate plant choice was not enough. Once the problem of 'what' was solved, the next step was 'how'. Gertrude Jekyll's Colour Schemes for the Flower Garden was a revelation. Her ghost tapped me on the shoulder and tugged at my sleeve. It was divine intervention. Her spirit-voice whispered: 'Untangle the chaos. Blend. Match. Harmonise. Consider colour, foliage and form. Capture a mood. Be bold. It's not so much what you put in but what you leave out. Try a bit of restraint Paula.' I got her drift. My garden plans levitated. Colour schemes captured my imagination. Gardening took on a new dimension as I adapted and coastalised her ideas of visual harmony with disciple devotion.

I saw the light. I was converted. The cottage garden was born again. Though still read as one large picture, with religious fervour it was divided into three compartments and planted with the chosen ones. Hedges of privet, *Ligustrum ovalifolium aureum* and *Lonicera nitida*, defined the boundaries.

I discovered that dense plantings and colour repetition of even ordinary plants can create extraordinary effects. Gathering in threes and fives and sevens and more, all-on-their-lonesomes have banded together. It's a joined-forces team effort. The close-knit groups of like-minded neighbours hit it off. Some go hungry. Others get by on just a snack in spring. As for a drink, most of them hardly touch the stuff.

Coordinated schemes were all the rage. I became colour conscious. Mix-and-match. This-goes-with-that. The winter garden stood like a dressmaker's dummy waiting to be dressed. Sharp winds cut out shapes. Beds tried on different outfits for size. Small, medium and extra-large plants were dragged from pillar to post to see how they fitted. First in were not best dressed. Some just weren't cut out for it and were scrapped to the ragbag.

There were no designer labels or accessories. It wasn't the latest up-to-the-minute style or the hottest gear. Nothing from the top-drawer. The plain Janes and fashion fuddy duddies were a bit dated to be in vogue. Dumpy daturas. Frumpy euphorbias. Gawky globe flowers. More coastal couture than garden glam. It's not an all-year good look. Some combos are fashion disasters but the gear is durable, well cut and heat resistant.

The cottage garden is a fashion victim. It switches outfits to suit the season. Through spring she's all frocked-up gadding about in a showy off-the-rack citrus and denim blue floral number. As the weather warms she slips into a loose-fitting mauve-white cotton sundress that could do with a wash. Tight corset hedges hold in a bulging midriff. Padded shoulders. Big hair. In high heels, she struts onto the catwalk, reeking of perfume. In negligeed twilight she squeezes into a backless, full-length silver lurex gown that trails the paths.

She glows in early autumn: wine-flushed cheeks and plum-coloured lip gloss. Wet leaves in cropped hair stiff with sea spray. She's touched up the black roots. Blonde to brunette: Copper Sunset, Henna Highlight or Midnight Muscatel hair-dye, blow-waved by the wind. Rain freshens her face. Sea mist moisturises her skin. Metallic-fleck flares, worn through at the knee, billow in the breeze. A seed-beaded blouse nipped in at the waist. She's lost weight. She's all partied out. She needs a make over. Manicure. Pedicure. Shave. Split ends could do with a trim. On autumn's last weekend she lets it all hang out.

For winter she claims, 'Nothing to wear.' Fewer clothes and no make-up expose her high cheekbones. Cruel winds give away facial lines. She's dragged out a retro number. A not-quite-in-style, picked up from an end-of-season clearance sale. Her slip's showing. She's wearing odd socks, inside out. Sensible shoes. Her hair's gone grey. Under astrakhan clouds she's wind-worn and leggy in a skimpy slit skirt and water-stained top. Low-cut, see-through, pre-shrunk, two sizes too small. Rather revealing. More grunge than hip.

The garden retains its casual charm. I still get it wrong, half-right or not quite right. But generally, colours blend and lines flow. It's easy on the eyes. Combinations vary but stay with cool-the-blood colours for summer. When cheeky annuals scribbled their way out of picture, (poppies are the most defiant) I used to rub them out as a faux pas in the painting. Though it might get me a slap on the hand from Ms Jekyll, these days I enjoy them for their untamed touch. Most plants have been weaned off water. It's not a show-off year-round feature but peaks in mid-spring to early summer.

Bed One: Lemons, Blues and Apricots

Shrubs, roses, perennials and free-seeding annuals combine with silver plants. Stoic shrubs take a back seat in the borders. Pride of Madeira *Echium candicans*' bold blue cylinders and spiky leaves blend with the euphorbias. Wattlebirds hang upside down on the sandy-coloured Chinese lantern, Abutilon Sydney Belle and apricot Abutilon Halo that hang-in-there in sun or semi-shade. *Rosa frühlingsgold* pales to primrose as it ages. Its lemon-cream saucers partner Golden Wings' single cups.

Blue salvias, ageratum and rosemary Blue Lagoon hedging act as shadowy contrasts to the lemons. Yellow chamomile *Anthemis tinctoria* E.C. Buxton's pale daisies match up with perennial sage *Phlomis russeliana*'s heart-shaped leaves and tiered lemon flowers. *Sisyrinchium striatum*'s strappy leaves shoot blood-streaked buds and straw-yellow flowers. *Achillea* Moonshine's primrose sprays and *Achillea* Salmon Beauty go hand-in-hand with torch lily *Kniphofia* Little Maids' cream torches. Blue-grey iris fans throw fat buds that open out to floppy blue petals.

Silvers thread the picture together. Silky *Artemisia ludoviciana*, *Artemisia absinthium* and everlasting *Helichrysum petiolare* light up the lemons. Tanacetum's fine-cut foliage is as decorative as cast-iron verandah lace. Lamb's ears, *Stachys byzantina*, fringe the beds. The luminous silvers lift the warm salmon roses Apricot Nectar and flamboyant Just Joey.

Biennial foxgloves should be on the coastal plants black list. They contradict the concept of 'right plant right place'. But they are my love interest on the side. I treat them as an annual plaything so the fling's over by the time summer jilts them. Foxgloves need a good feed but have to cadge a drink from spring rains. Vertical foxglove spires and opium poppies grab the limelight to cast a spell of spring magic. *Digitalis purpurea* Sutton's Apricot flowers dotted all around the stem are lusher than the one-sided pink-throated flowers. The floral bells silently tinkle between the apricot roses and splashed yellow-blue Dutch iris.

Annuals scatter seeds around. Such charming pictures happen more by chance than planning. Borage, *Borago officinalis*, pops up all over the place. Love-in-the-mist, *Nigella damascena*, frames blue-haze blooms. Patches of crackling, papery seed pods decorate the apricot rose beds for weeks.

Bed Two: Yellows and Plums

Chilean buddleia, *Buddleia globosa*, throws honey-yellow balls that bounce around in late spring winds. The Himalayan *Buddleia crispa*'s musky pink flowers are nothing to brag about. Its true claim to fame is silvered felt foliage that deepens after flowering. It forms a striking backdrop to lift the yellows and plum-mauve poppies.

Euphorbias hack the heat. *Euphorbia wulfenii*'s triffid heads and lime-green and yellow eyes stare across late winter-early spring beds. Its sombre leaves set off summer sages, yarrows, anthemis and the lemon-peppery pea flowers of the tree lupin, *Lupinus arboreus*.

Sedums go great-guns in the sand and are practically bulletproof. Sedums, cardoons and wormwoods cool the contrasting barberry, *Berberis thunbergii*, cannas and aeoniums' maroons and burgundies. Grey-green-leaved roses complement the bush background. *Rosa glauca*'s deep pink blooms and arching habit match *Rosa* Reine de Violette's carmine flowers and glaucous leaves.

Yuccas are teetotallers, toughing out drought without a drop. Succulents are non-drinkers. Echeverias scalloped rosettes stay sober through drink-dry summers. Spoonbills seesaw on the stems of waxy pink blooms.

Yarrows team up with Jerusalem sage *Phlomis russeliana*'s buttery tiers. Yarrows' plate-shaped bunches can let the side down whenever rabbits get the chance to serve themselves. Valerian *Centranthus ruber's* fleshy leaves and cerise flower heads weave their way through the yellows. Dyer's chamomile *Anthemis tinctoria*'s brilliant yellow daisies hug the front of the bed.

Strings of self-sowers tie the pictures together. White parasols of Queen Anne's Lace shade under-planted honesty *Lunaria annua*'s cream-variegated leaves and white opium poppies.

The sky is overcast this late spring morning. Cloud curdles west off Bass Strait. Rose, opium and buddleia perfumes weight the warm air. Pot-bellied bees stagger from poppy to poppy. Dried-out leaves crackle like cellophane in my fist. Wrens pip-a-peep. Flycatchers twitter about. Freshly opened flowers glow in the diffused light.

I breast-stroke through an ocean of cornflowers and ageratum, frothed white with cabbage moths. Backlit flowers are translucent. Gold rim light filters through Queen Anne's Lace doilies. I drown in a sea of scent as I bend to gather a garland of roses for my friend Jude. Long-stemmed blooms are reminiscent of faded needlework. The rose stalks are wet and shiny with dew. On such long legs they'll hold their heads up high in any vase. The snip of the secateurs cuts the silence. Primrose, buttercup yellow, wine-purple and crimson-stained buds will open out to ragbag blooms in water. The roses spill over my arms. Sheets of damp newspaper will ease bruising and wilting in the car.

Bed Three: Whites and Mauves

In hard heat silvers seem metal heavy. The colour palette smudges. Flowers wilt and droop. Petals fade. But in the early morning and evening, mauves, chalky whites and silvers keep their cool. Alliums and catmint's milky-mauves are reflected in the native star-flowered kangaroo apple, *Solanum aviculare*. Midsummer's white tree poppies, gaura, roses and cosmos imitate sweet bursaria's white puffs powdered along the coast.

Buddleias are a mecca for tortoiseshell butterflies. Honeyeaters swing on the stems and bury their beaks into *Buddleia davidii alba* and *Buddleia* White Bouquet's nectar-filled blossoms. These sturdy shrubs need post-flower butchering or their posture slumps.

Californian tree poppy, *Romneya coulteri*, is at home by the sea, though it prefers to lead a sheltered life protected from winds. It is tricky to strike from cuttings but sends up shoots out of the blue. Fried-egg flowers frisbee around in high winds soaking the summer garden with an erotic scent. Its glaucous foliage and fuzzy, yellow-haired buds are flattering features. In the evening, the flowers close to pearl-white scallop shells.

Abutilon vitifolium's powdery sage-green leaves hint at hardiness, but while settling in, it craves a drink after a long day. The white form, Album, swamps the shrubs with flat blossoms from September and works flexi-time as a backdrop for the white roses. *Rosa alba maxima*'s blooms lead a double life. Its coarse grey-green leaves blend in so they can't be recognised. *Rosa rugosa alba*'s single-minded flowers glow white among wrinkly foliage. The leaves tend to sun-scorch but it is trouble-free.

Towards the back of the border, gone-up-in-the-world perennials rub shoulders with white roses. Night-scented tobacco *Nicotiana tabacum*'s after-dark perfume drifts head-high through the garden. Its white tubular flowers are magnetic to honeyeaters. Spinebills and crescent honeyeaters drink from the long flutes. Sticky, bright green leaves splatter black with insects. It tends to be a bossy britches and push its way around if not kept in line. *Macleaya cordata* towers to two metres without water. Lobed leaves mimic palms. Creamy panicles glisten white before turning rust-gold.

Biennial clary sage, *Salvia sclarea* var. *turkestanica*, works after hours as a perennial in the mild conditions. Its musky leaves seem sugar coated. Lavender spires complement the white roses. Sun-loving *Gaura lindheimeri*'s long-lasting wands flutter with cabbage-moth flowers. Sea campion, *Silene maritima*, dresses in period costume. It wears curious green-white lace-edged bonnets for weeks. It can be an over achiever. Lanky suckers sneak around where they are not wanted and need to be watched. Rose campion *Lychnis coronaria alba*'s white flowers run on empty when the going gets tough. Eye-high elephant or Russian garlic, *Allium ampeloprasum*, pushes up through the perennials. Pom-pom mauve flowers stand tall until winds knock them flat.

Catmint, *Nepeta* x *faassenii*, is a quiet achiever. It keeps a low profile tumbling over the retaining walls for weeks on end. Its big sister, *Nepeta* Six Hill's Giant, is a real workhorse. To trim faded stalks, Margery Fish suggests, 'The best way to do this is to work from below. Lift up the lady's skirts and cut all the old growth from underneath.' New shoots spring up from the centre of the plant into a succession of fresh blooms.

Clean white sheets of cosmos are thrown over grubby beds. Patches are sown so thickly the plants prop each other up. Feathery strands and white daisies flap about in summer winds and steal the show for weeks until pack-a-punch autumn gales snap off side stems and knock the stuffing out of them.

Traditionally, dahlias were true cottage garden plants, often edging a path or potato bed. I have taken a shine to cactus dahlias. Colour matches of white, lemon and apricot stretch out the season. Although dahlias binge on food and drink and are deadhead dependent to come up with continuous flowers, this gluttony rewards us with basket loads of precise-shaped blooms.

Cut bunches of summer dahlias combined with crepey cosmos and starry leek and acid-yellow dill seed heads reflect the gardens colours. Bronze-leaved dahlias' shaggy, fluted and furled coppery blooms give a polished performance, rubbing up against each other in a brass vase by the window.

When summer grows long in the tooth, the cottage garden takes over. There's no stopping it. Dahlias disobey orders to stand up straight. Cosmos collapse. Lonicera loll about. Ligustrum let their hair down. Button seeds pop open. Box lets out its belt a few notches and breathes easier. Hedges loosen the ties on their straight jackets and go mad. Weeds get a life. Couch grass runs riot. Secateurs are missing and who cares. Clippers gather dust. The head gardener looks the other way. She admits defeat and stops playing control freak. She cops out in a cane chair, puts her feet up, kicks back with a book and loses the day.

Withered seed heads and tattered blooms can make the garden look ratty after a long, hot summer. Autumn pictures are brief. *Sedum* Autumn Joy's rust tones, cardoon thistle heads, terracotta yarrow, late apricot roses and bronzy dahlias repeat the salt marsh's russet club rush, claret glasswort and gold banksia cone colours. Silver eyes tightrope along fallen stems, pecking at cardoon thistle and euphorbia seed heads.

Aeonium zwartkop and cannas show their dark sides. Burgundy foliage, macleaya's brassy feather-duster seed heads, tree poppies' bristly gold buds and silvers set off rose flushes. Money bags honesty is filthy-rich with coin-filled seed purses. Freshly minted seeds splurge their life's savings. They are big spenders with small change until winter sends them broke.

The end of autumn means an overhaul. Work tackled now keeps me one jump ahead in spring. I turn into a razor-gang of one, sharpening shears and getting plants into shape. Misbehaving hedges that have wandered off the straight and narrow are snipped into line. Clippers scissor cheeky crew cuts, smooth shapes and cut cushions to echo windblown beach topiary. Rose stems get the chop. Frost-blackened dahlias are dug. Past-their-prime perennials are cut back. Clumps are broken up. Those too big for their boots are cut down to ankle-length , ready to fill spring's shoes.

After working spring and summer's double shift, the cottage garden is laid off in late autumn and winter. Gaps advertise vacancies. The gardener feels like handing in her notice. Textures and foliage come to the fore rather than the focus of flowers. Chrome-silver plants' reputation is dented in winter as they seem dull under gloomy skies but the silvers act as a steel frame. The bond between the garden and landscape is enhanced. Harmonies and contrasts with the bush are even more pleasing. With few flowers on show, the silveriness becomes a colour feature in itself.

Winter goes minimalist. The garden's frame is exposed. I look through the keyhole and enter through the back door left open. The house is vacant. The outdoor rooms need renovating: a dust-off, paint job, repairs on faulty workmanship and bad plumbing. The drains are clogged with leaves. Rain drips down windowpanes. The cold tap's running. A puddle is spilt on the floor. Fold-up flowers are packed away in dresser drawers, hung in wardrobes and suitcases or stuffed in the laundry basket to come out crumpled in spring. Vases are empty. The fruit bowl is bare. The table is cleared.

Nature plays interior decorator. She's spot-on with the décor. A tasteful choice from the coastal colour chart: sky blue–grey ceiling, tea-tree green wallpaper in a banksia motif with a matt finish and a wood-panelled feature wall. Rooms with a view are fitted out with comfortable floor coverings woven with natural fibres: a moss-green rug thrown over a leaf-patterned wall-to-wall carpet in earth tones. Sandstone tiles.

I refurbish the rooms: re-upholster the worn bits with secateurs, vinyl-wet, leatherette leaves and straw sofa-soft. I strip unmade beds, air the mattresses, tuck in fitted sheets and pile on extra blankets until the rooms are livable.

Winter brings in the demolition crew. Rain ruins the carpet. Home-wrecker winds mess up beds, break frames, bang shutters, knock on doors, rattle knobs and whistle draughts through wall cracks.

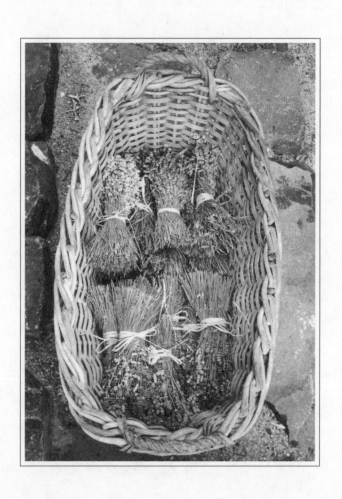

ROSES, POPPIES AND LAVENDER

Roses have a reputation. Temperamental in coastal gardens. But I wouldn't listen to hearsay. I was gaga for Graham Thomas, dippy about Duke of Edinburgh and head-over-heels for Hugh Dickson. I was smitten with Satchmo, lusted for Lawrence Johnston and had recurring dreams about Doctor Deakin (Edward to his friends). My love was truly madly deeply, and there was no turning back.

Roses played hard to get. Wallabies nibbled leaves. Flowers gave up in the sand. Maybe they weren't my type, after all, we scarcely knew each other. I was inexperienced. We were having problems. Heartbroken, I called the whole thing off. Once the fence came between us though, I was hell-bent on getting me and roses back together. It was more than a crush. I wanted more than a one-night stand.

The next time round I was choosy. I went for the strong, silent type. Partners with personality and character: hardy, disease-resistant, flower-generous and how they got along with the neighbours (even those two doors down). Physical attraction, beauty, brand of perfume, leaf, fruit and habit were lower on the checklist.

I planned our future together. I did some groundwork. It was our getting-to-know-you phase. In autumn I dug bare-rooted plants into deep compost making sure they were comfortable. This gave the roots time to settle in. Soil was firmed into a mound at the base to anchor and ease wind damage. I lavished affection, spreading wilted comfrey between fresh sheets of newspapers and straw in sunny, well-made beds. Food and drink were on hand when they needed it. Love blossomed.

Roses are demanding, but it's give and take, good times and bad. Flowers can be a bit off-colour by the end of the season but we stay together in sickness and in health. Snipping twiggy summer growth fights black spot. Leaves are sometimes spotted black but not enough for concern. Aphids are squashed by hand. Good air circulation keeps fungal disease at bay. Comfrey's potash helps ripen new wood. Mulch cuts down complaints. Blooms blush a deeper colour on the bush and in the vase.

We go our separate ways in summer. Passion fades. Weekend water visits are our only contact. Though some get a bit touchy, I am not precious with pruning. When the Icebergs run out of steam, I hack off their heads with the clippers. Ringtails chew on clematis and young vine leaves but so far the roses have proved possum-proof.

Roses leave me in winter but we keep in touch. There's no love lost. We're fair-weather friends. But absence makes the heart grow fonder. Then it's on-again off-again. It runs hot and cold. We have our ups and downs. It's not a full-on affair. We're not always faithful to each other. Sometimes we're just not interested. It's a thorny relationship. The honeymoon's over. But when roses send me spring bouquets, scatter he-loves-me, he-loves-me-not petals at my feet and gift-wrap autumn perfumes that go straight to my head, I know we'll always be more than just good friends.

Red Rose Garden

The brief was simple: a red rose garden enclosed by hedged stone walls where we could lounge and sip champagne on summer evenings.

The orchard, vegetable garden and cottage garden were in full swing. It was time to go beyond the functional to the frivolous, to wallow in the delights of red and elegance of silver. This garden goes off the boil in winter but runs red-hot through the remaining seasons.

The rose shades are darker and more heavy-hearted than the Flanders poppy. These duskier tones absorb light and heat and suit the close range and intimate viewing. The banksia backdrop subdues and dapple-shades the roses so they keep a cool head in a heat crisis.

The picket gate scrapes across stone pavers. Curry plant *Helichrysum italicum*'s peppery curry, cumin and fenugreek perfume lures me in. There are two forms of this plant. I mistakenly combined them both but the duotones weave the silver edging together. The less compact and longer, stickier leaves makes clipping clumsier than on the shorter form. The neutral tone contrasts with the red roses and highlights them as rubies set in silver.

Red roses fill the four rectangular beds. I stoop and sniff each head-spinning scent. The tall, dark and handsome Mr Lincoln's buds open to a mouth of satin red lips. Hot-tempered Deuil de Paul Fontaine's buds unfold to open-hearted maroon cups studded in a crown of gold stamens. Full-bodied Etoile de Holland's flushed cheeks fade to crimson velvet. Josephine Bruce's blushed complexion shows off her brilliant stamens.

Chive baubles dot the beds. Though chives are so-called companion plants for roses, new shoots and bud tips are usually crawling with aphids. Dead-heading and blood and bone pick-me-ups spur on blooms.

Sparks fly as dahlias firecracker like Catherine wheels igniting the summer picture. Cactus dahlias, Mrs Rees, slow-burn red. May Johnson's quill-shaped petals burst into flames. Autumn rekindles the fire. Rain douses the blaze.

In late afternoon light, pintucked pom-pom dahlias stand like matches waiting to be struck. Smoky liquorice leaves tone down Bishop of Llandaff's and Fire Mountain's' scarlets. Inky-bronze foliage casts its black magic. Dark-leaf dahlias can be hard to come by on the 'black' market so I take cuttings from late spring shoots.

Perilla frutescens mulberry leaves cool the burning reds. It resembles Purple Ruffles' basil, tastes of aniseed but is not as pungent. As summer heats up, the ruffled leaves glint tinsel-gold. All this from one original plant I bought for fifty cents from an Inverloch elderly citizen's club fete. Cheap thrills.

Reds strike a contrast with the glossy green lonicera hedge wrapped around this garden. Lime-green dill lightens the dark shades. Self-sewn bronze fennel's feather dusters soften the straitlaced rose stems.

Colours hot up at late-in-the-day dusk when shadows lengthen. On the stone seat we bask in the blood-warm sunset. Glass stems glitter. A cork pops. Crystal clinks. The sea serenades. We soak up the warmth of the stone, drink in the perfumes and tingle of chilled champagne.

Poppies

Poppies are one of the garden year's highlights. In early spring, Iceland poppies, *Papaver nudicaule*, waver on spindly stems above apple-green leaves. Single pastel-flesh, ivory-cream, salmon and lemon crepe cups seem sewn with invisible thread. The poppies appear fragile yet somehow manage to keep body and soul together through needle-sharp rains and winds. Iceland poppies are not as hardy here as other poppies and rarely spread their own seed. The flowers compose a three-dimensional watercolour in a clear glass vase. Right before my eyes, cashmere buds raise their heads in slow motion, split and open out. Petals float above hairy stems as flexible as florists' wire. In a day or two, petals flutter to the floor.

Late spring, I wade waist-high through a sea of opium poppies, *Papaver somniferum*. Ruffled blooms and seed heads drench the garden with the peculiar opium odour. Tipsy bees taste from plum, grape and wine-coloured silver-stemmed chalices. Seeds spill from blue goblets. Hypnotised by bee-drone I lounge along the stone wall, hazy with catmint. Poppies are dressed to kill in dusky Pink Chiffon, maroon-black Black Paeony that fades to mauve and the unusual White Cloud that my dear friend Jean gave me from her Warragul garden.

Wild poppies wear a single lilac skirt stained purple. Swollen buds burst, split open at the sides and release silk balloons. A breeze tousles pom-pom heads as they perform centre stage in their stint as stars in a brief but dazzling career.

The poppies flirt, flaunting tutus. In a trick of the light they spin. Dance of the sugar plum fairies. The poppies can-can, swishing hitched-up crumpled skirts, lifting raggy petticoats, kicking up silver-stockinged legs head high.

As the season fades, winds rip seed heads open. Seeds spurt into cracks between stones. The top-heavy weights become punching bags for sparring winds that strike them out cold. Gales bite their heads off. Blade-sharp rains shred the pulpy leaves and disposable petals. Torn blooms litter the beds like scrunched-up trash. The breeze throws away the bits of loose-leaf paper.

The wild corn poppy, *Papaver rhoeas*, is a symbol of remembrance of those who died at Flanders in France during the First World War. Flanders poppies and their cultivar Shirley poppies are free-flowering ferals. Whiskered buds unfold to medal-shiny, bloodstained sheets of poppies that trickle down onto paths. Sunrise is a reincarnation as red as a Remembrance Day picnic. Red-cloth flowers flap in the breeze like victory flags. Some wave at half-mast. Against a khaki backdrop the poppies battle the heat, stand to attention and soldier on through November until surrendering to summer's farewell salute.

Summer mops up the last drops. Bled dry, the garden pales into anaemia until next spring's transfusion. Wind blows them to pieces. It buries the wounded. Dried pods resemble urns scattering ash-fine seed dust to dust. My fingers crush corpses. Stems shatter in my hands. In winter daydreams, poppies burn my mind in remembrance.

Summer-flowering Californian poppy *Eschscholzia californica*'s dissected blue-green feathers and silky orange or cream flowers shimmer with a sheen impossible to paint. In thirst-crazed heat it spills seeds, edging paths and joins in with calendulas to splash colour through the vegetables.

The Welsh poppy, *Meconopsis cambrica*, wears a peach-coloured mini-skirt. It is quieter and frailer than the papavers. This simplicity is its true charm. Deeply divided ferny foliage throws up long-stemmed single flowers. The poppy pops up goodness-knows-where-ever it can find a drink.

Flanders, opium and Californian poppies all thrive on malnutrition. Coastal thin soil and a starvation diet appear perfect. The poppies are a lazy-bone gardener's dream. No planting, no feeding, no watering. It's sit-back-and-watch-them-grow gardening. I gather bunches in bud and plunge the stems into boiling water to seal the ends. Poppies are enduring cut flowers.

Lavender

When I finally twigged that selecting silver plants was part of the solution to 'getting it right' on the coast, I gained confidence. I sketched out a design for a circular lavender garden that could be looked down on from the upstairs room in the cottage.

Lavender is quintessential to coastal gardens. It comes with credentials. It's an all-time great and a seaside success. Once established, it's in for the summer-long haul. It revels in the open, drained, sun-baked soil and basks in the high temperatures. Pebbles and stone steps snare the sun's warmth and draw out its oily scent. We turn off the taps and give watering a miss.

Chinese juniper, *Juniperus chinensis hibernica,* frame the cottage. We lashed out and bought these as advanced trees. The investment paid off with long-term gains. The trees gave an instant ageing. Prickly silver needles blend with the bush and even under the eaves the trees hold on through the dry. Their solid, shadowy form sets off the Iceberg rose hedges that run parallel to the low stone walls.

Wisteria *floribunda alba* twists its way around the pergola's posts. In spring it drips with lilac-flushed bunches of floral grapes and it shades the pergola all summer. French lavender, *Lavandula dentata*, hedges border the fence lines. Regular clipping gets them into shape. Lilac spikes of English lavender, *Lavandula officinalis*, frame the quarter circles.

Bulbs are renowned for blooming in cooler climates away from the coast. But some that originate from the Mediterranean and South Africa have adjusted to this drier coastal garden. The few bulbs I shoved in one autumn years ago have gone forth and multiplied despite my neglect to split the clumps on a regular basis. Spring's starry scillas, white bluebells, grape hyacinths and even goblets of the dry-tolerant Monet white tulips have naturalised under the olive trees. Battalions of jonquils and daffodils, Erlicheer, Silver Chimes and Paper White march into spring. Pheasant's eye, *Narcissus poeticus*, is always the last to flower if it manages to hold its head up to winds travelling at break-neck speed. The silver-whites blend with the flowering tea-tree's backdrop.

White liliums scent under the pergola. Liliums prefer a richer and moister soil than this garden can offer so the Christmas lily, *Lilium longiflorum*, and the purple-tinged regal lily, *Lilium regale*, are pampered in terracotta tubs. I bow down to the sweet breath, almost kissing the wax-lips of a flower's mouth. Staggered planting gives armfuls of blooms just before, during and after Christmas.

Our crescent-shaped sickle is rusty but sharp. It's handy for harvesting lavender when oils are at their peak just before flowering. I bend-bunch-cut, bend-bunch-cut, sawing clock-wise around the circle and stuffing the washing basket full. My fingertips brush the scented hedges, pinching and bruising the leaves. My bare feet crush the confetti flower carpets and mats of woolly thyme, creeping through the paving. In the cottage I bundle bunches and bind with purple bows. Bouquets dangle from the rafters.

Outside the circle, to the north, clipped lavender cotton curves between semi-circular stone steps. The climbing rose Mme Alfred Carriere scrambles over the stone duck house. Though slow to take off in the semi-shade, its fragrant white-flushed pink flowers waft through the spicy scents. The white rose The Nun spills perfume from chalices. Fallen petals resemble communion bread. In autumn it is beaded with a rosary of hips.

Olive trees seem at home in the grey-green landscape. The trees repeat the colour, shape and texture of the corky-barked banksias and balance the curved stone seats either side of the gate. Olive trees put up with sandy soils but a good feed when flowers pop open and fruit is forming, gives a higher yield.

YELLOW GARDEN

Coastal light is startlingly bright. We are drenched in white light reflected from the sea. This light changes through the seasons. Summer light can be garish and glary. Low sun and longer shadows soften autumn light. Winter light is highly tuned. Spring's light is clear.

Seasonal changes and light affect colour in the garden. When sunlight strengthens, brighter primary colours blaze. Spring's accentuated yellows and greens lift the spirits after winter. During late spring to summer, though, the cooler, pastel tones refresh. Autumn's golds and tans stand out. Metallic silvers shine. In winter, silvers lose their lustre.

Colours are more luminous on overcast days when the bush is blanketed in low cloud. When cloud cover lifts, light bounces off foliage and flowers, bleaching colours, outlining shadows and defining light and dark.

The landscape has influenced my colour choice. Wattles, banksias, hibbertia and senecio flowers come in assorted shades of yellow. Bursaria, leucopogon, tea-tree, boobialla, sambucus and correa flaunt a range of whites. Reds are reflected in the salt marsh's crimson glasswort and sea berry saltbush *Atriplex cinerea*'s squashed red fruits that stain fingers blood-purple.

Colours are combined with silvers that subdue schemes and act as go-betweens, linking the cultivated garden with the surrounds. Coordinating colour schemes is touch-and-go. Garden pictures are ephemeral (though this is part of the delight and a reminder of life's transience). It's tricky manipulating cliché-free combinations that hang together when they're supposed to. There's so much to mull over: colour, contrast, foliage, texture, height, width, rhythm, repetition. Not to mention timing. It's hard to pull it off. It takes experimenting, making adjustments, planning and practice. It means having a good geek in similar-climate gardens (such as at Heronswood, Dromana) where they get it right. It also takes a fair whack of luck.

My first tries were fizzers. Even when I copycatted from books, the play-it-safe carbon copies fell short of the picturesque lookalikes. I got adventurous, aimed at grand colour-scapes and still misfired. But in time I came up with my own roughly-at-the-same-time compositions and I discovered the joy of making more than 'happy accidents'. There's always room for improvement. I lie in bed dreaming up knock-em-dead and you-ain't-seen-nothin-yet schemes. Rules can always be broken. The sky's the limit.

It's still early days. I will be a long time serving my apprenticeship. So far it's never been a case of eat-your-heart-out Monet. But my paintbox is smaller now and my brush strokes are broader. I scumble on colour and work it in to the canvas, toning and overlapping shapes. It's even more fun than puddling a paintbrush in water, sweeping it across the paint book washed landscapes from my childhood. I now dare to go over the lines, to break the frame so plants spill off the page free-style.

Mother nature joins in. Her pictures are unplanned and

spontaneous. Flicking seeds, tinting and toning, she can be as hard to pin down as her can't-catch-hold-of pictures. She throws in unpredictable weather just to keep you on your toes. She calls the shots, keeps you guessing and makes the final brush strokes. We are at her mercy.

The cottage garden's in-the-long-run success taught me to think twice before tackling any new garden. By the time we got round to the space between the vegetable and cottage garden, we nutted it out carefully. Autumn-spring's silver banksias flushed with gold cones inspired the choice of yellow.

This garden room is sheltered to the north and south by low stone walls. *Lonicera nitida* hedges have been slow to settle in. Espaliered nashi trees screen picket fences east and west. Summer-autumn's russet-skinned fruits blend with the yellow-based scheme.

Yellow is cheery after winter gloom and early spring's few-and-far-between fine days. Changing light affects yellow more than any other colour. Brighter summer sun turns gold to brass. Muted autumn sun tends to mellow gold leaves and flowers. But in spring when the sun is lower and the light is softer, yellows sparkle.

Herbs suit the dry site. Yellow-splashed sage, *Salvia officinalis icterina,* and clipped southernwood, *Artemisia abrotanum*, circle a central chimney pot. Lad's love looks shabby through the cold weather but scrubs up well after a dose of spring sun and a haircut. Lavender cotton, *Santolina chamaecyparissus*, sets off the citrus shades and frames the beds as canvases for living pictures. It demands spring clippings but summer stops it in its tracks.

The wallflowers were a fluke. On the spur of the moment I cast their fate to the wind when I tossed out some seeds on site one autumn. Carpets of pointy-leaved seedlings sprang up in spring. Wallflowers turned out to be tough customers when mulched and wind-protected. *Cheiranthus cheiri* Fire King and the primrose Moonlight's egg-and-bacon, mahogany, caramel and cadmium suit the stone walls' rusty tones. Wallflowers stick it out for weeks. Dead-heading with the clippers gives more-to-come and keeps the plants compact.

Velvet wallflowers make an eye-catching contrast with terracotta poppy Orange Chiffon's papery petals and grey-blue leaves. Petals are now and again blotched black at the base. The poppies, at home in the bone-dry soil, glow like sunlit lamps until short-circuited by summer. Serrated seed heads shake out pepper seeds.

Californian poppies lap up the limelight. Silky cups and steely-blue foliage diffuse the yellows and carry colour into summer. Roses run a relay passing the baton on to one another. Gold Bunny and Freesia's clear, wavy flowers bloom their heads off from spring through to autumn. *Rosa* Graham Thomas climbs its way through the garden house trellis. Flowers open to buttery cups and breathe a hint of fresh tea.

Dahlias dazzle from summer to autumn. Yellow Hammer and Moonfire's chocolate-black foliage and lime-yellow flowers partner the poppies. The roses and dahlias are mulched with dried manure, dead-headed and soaked weekly during the summer peak.

In spring sun, yellows gleam with gold. The garden shines, brimming with light. An ibis honks overhead as I relax with a cuppa. My companion, a semi-tame yellow robin, clamped on the rim of the chimney pot, joins me. I gather an armful of dew-wet wallflowers and yellow rosebuds and plunge them up to their necks in a bucket of warm water. Inside I am a florist with flair, stripping stems and filling green glass vases.

THE NATIVE GARDEN

The native garden is a bush extension. It's a wild backyard. Originally we planted this area around the house with introduced natives. Grevilleas and correas lured honeyeaters but changed the distinctive coastal bush.

Over the years we've come to respect and work with plants already present. Shrubs have been replaced with squat indigenous species bought from local native plant nurseries that collect and propagate local seed. We have come full circle. Nature not nurture. Strawy clumps of knobby club rush have naturalised. Native elderberry *Sambucus gaudichaidiana*'s pale-green stems hang creamy-white flower clusters in spring. Its musky scent weaves its way through the tapestry of grey-greens. These plants blend with the landscape, thrive in the local conditions and create a unique garden, not an imposed design. My next-time-round coastal garden would feature indigenous plants.

Some of the native coastal plants respond to clipping. Cushion bush *Calocephalus brownii*'s tangled mound of silver twigs trims up well. Coastal rosemary, *Westringia fruticosa*

Wynabbie gem form, tea-tree, *Leptospermum laevigatum* and coastal correa *Correa alba*'s grey flannel foliage shear to dense topiary hedging.

This garden is a wildlife meeting place. It's a neighbourhood habitat. Communal living in hidey-hole homes. Scorpions scuttle under rocks. Ants trail through twigs. Sand beetles crawl across leaf litter. Spinebills hover like hummingbirds, dipping bills into correa bowls. Splintery songs, high-pitched 'tiziz tiziz', 'prip prip' and rosella 'ping' peal through the garden. Blue-tongue lizards drag their bellies through the mulch or sunbake in stony corners. The children entice them inside to lick jam-stained spoons with stretchy blue tongues. Spined echidnas resemble walking cactus as they waddle through the birdbaths, probing for bull ants.

From the verandah I watch a pair of tuxedoed magpies strutting around, cracking their beaks and daggering the lawn. Our pet maggie Stickybeak stabs his cheese breakfast from the kitchen table. Wailing and screechy voices announce the arrival of yellow-tailed black cockatoos. In open areas the birds tear bark for grubs, grind banksia seeds then float off with slow creaking wing beats, sinister silhouettes in the smoky-blue dusk.

Sun highlights Christmas beetles' gold-bronze shine and aqua sheen. The beetles blunder along an erratic flight path like flying opals. As a child I set them as brooches in cotton-woolled matchboxes and rubbed the enamelled coat that felt as shiny as a polished fingernail.

Pygmy possums are only finger length. Sprawled out on the kitchen floor, they surrender to the heat. Pink brush-tipped tongues lap up watermelon juice from a well in my daughter Tshinta's hand. In the cooler evening, they launch themselves from a windowsill to frisk the nightscape for nectar and pollen, fruits and insects.

West of the house we scooped out a pond. The area's about seven by four metres and one metre deep. It was lined with black plastic, reinforced with chicken wire, cemented and edged with flat stones. At first it seemed a bit like a fake lake in a new housing estate. We waited a few weeks for the lime to settle, then introduced a few fish to their new home. The pond soon evolved its own ecosystem. When spring rains fell, jellied black eggs turned to tadpoles. Thornbill bark-thatched nests, home units with an overlooking-the-lake view, hung from hidden branches.

Run-off from the roof keeps the pond full. Summer's water level drops but it's deep enough to cater for populations of visiting wildlife. It's self-serve at the local watering hole. Kangaroos drop in for drinks. Firetails scoop up a sip. Poolside spinebills swoop and splash the shallows. Thrushes soak, ruffle feathers and ring-ripple the water. Thornbills torpedo, churn along, do a few laps and come up for breath. Fantails spray their wings. Willie wagtails and robins baptise themselves. Wattlebirds belly-whack. Honeyeaters dive bomb and splash about. Lace-winged dragonflies hover in a train linking tails with their mates. Herons-on-stilts stalk the shallows. Skinks flicker under rocks.

The pond provides eat-in dining or take-away food for families. Fantails dip their beaks and skim for mosquitoes. Kookaburras hang around in the dusty dry of late summer hoping to make a meal of a snake, lizard or frog. The aquatic native nardoo *Marsilea drummondii*'s floating four-leaf clovers and the feathery oxygenating weed *Myriophyllum aquaticum* are havens for fish, frogs, insects and water snails and cut down the spread of algae. Floating banksia leaves screen speckled fish. In warm weather I trawl the rake through the green slime choked with twigs from fallen branches.

In spring sun, baby joeys are out and about and feeling frisky.

Satin-pink heads peep from bulky pouches. Lanky-limbed and lop-sided, testing pogo-stick hind legs, the young never venture far from their mothers. We are protective of our new babies, keeping an eye out for foxes. The joeys tame easily with no dogs and cats around. The kids name them Joeyhoey or Jeau.

Kangaroos are family orientated and move around in mobs. Our resident population is usually about three females, their joeys and older brothers and sisters. They shave fresh grass, lick their pelts, scratch their bellies with leathery hands, prick their ears and call to one another. Distinctive markings of white-tipped tails, colourings and facial expressions set individuals apart. Whenever we are away we miss their deep-set velvet eyes, dark lashes and gentle company.

It is thrilling to have such close encounters with wild creatures, to watch the comings and goings, to meet them eye to eye and to share their trust.

Terry and I straggle off in morning mist through banksia woodland to walk the tip of the Point. It's as if we are ships heading out to sea when a bronze-wing's 'oom oom' guides us like a foghorn.

Point Smythe is one of the largest sand spits in Victoria. It is shaped like a double-edged spear. The Inlet side supports a salt marsh community. Venus Bay's surf beaches and wind-ravaged dunes facing Bass Strait form a feeding corridor for the migratory birds.

Barley sugar tea-tree lean away from the wind. Seasoned trees shed bark. These bearded men are the senior citizens of the forest and can spiral to fifteen metres in old age. Bones creak as these muscle-limbed old-timers sigh and rub their hairy arms and thigh-thick trunks against each other. Crushed leaves smell of eucalypt and tea-tree oil. The vapour is heady in the heat. In the younger forest, stick figures lean towards the light. Spiders cast web-nets, laying traps between trunks. Caught in an invisible thread, a leaf spins.

Our feet sink into bog-peat. Drought dieback has skeletoned melaleucas to a cemetery of paperbark bones. Big blackwoods fringe the swamp. I rub my palm across a trunk, press my fingers in the furrowed bark and stroke the sun-buffed leaves. Banksias are curtained with downy clematis.

The air is sticky. Mozzies fizz around our faces flushed with heat. We slap ourselves stupid and smear lumpy bites with spit. Two bottlenose dolphins tumble through the shallows.

We scrabble over low dunes carpeted in sea rocket, strappy spinifex and the swollen lips of pigface. Grass tips draw arcs in the sand. Surf crashes. We stare out to the horizon line graffitied with cloud. Ocean and inlet merge, ripple-patterning the waters.

Seabirds meet on the shore tip. Breakers spread a white lace tablecloth. High tide eats the headland. Cliffs crumble. Seagulls squawk, shriek and strut about on stalky legs. Some sit paper napkin stiff, unfolding and flapping their serviette wings as they fly off ready to dine. Cormorants fan raggy wings dry. Pacific gulls 'awk-awk-awk' swinging in the breeze. Crested terns whirl, whistle and dart through the sky like arrows shot from a bow.

We backtrack along the surf beach. Wind combs marram grass dune heads. Sandpipers graze the tide line. The birds skitter through the wave wash, skate the glassy sand and fly off in rippling formation. Oyster catchers peep-a-peep. Sea gulls karr-karr-karr-keow riding the upside-down surf-sky for the billowing clouds resemble waves breaking in the blue.

The wind is spiced with salt. The beach is as-far-as-the-eye-can-see empty. Spinifex cartwheel in the wind. Catch-me-if-you-can waves chase us as we kick foam along the ocean's edge. Salt stains our trouser cuffs. Sand-speckled toes crunch shell grit. We pop seaweed pods. Sea snails doodle. Waves wipe the magic slate clean.

A low-gliding gull drags its shadow over us. The wind whistles through a bird skull embalmed in seagrass. It grinds bones to sand. We pick through beach bric-a-brac and castaway curios: sea-polished bird bones, weedy sea-dragons, feathers, cuttlefish, jellyfish, starfish, abalone shells, bladderwrack, shredded bait bags, an orange plastic buoy, sea grapes and kelp rags. Our fingers scuttle over hollowed crabs and claws, anemones and urchins, washed-up fishbones, driftwood, bits of blue nylon fishing net and stones tumbled smooth. Tide and winds have hurled these relics onto shore linking the ocean world with the land. Sandy periwinkles, broken chinaman's fingernails, cowries, cone shells and painted ladies we've gathered, rattle in my hat.

This hazardous stretch of sea has swallowed ships whole. It seems haunted by ghosts of drowned seamen and explorers such as George Bass who first sighted Venus Bay in 1798. We stagger home exhausted to welcome the shelter of our garden. In a jam jar on the window sill, the sun-varnished shells shine in water.

COURTYARD

The courtyard is an open-air hideaway. It's a sky-roofed room hugged on three sides by gone-grey paling fences and adjoining cottage. Terracotta-tubbed citrus trees add an Italianate touch.

Four double-grafted Meyer-Lisbon trees sting the air with the tang of lemon blossom. The compact Meyer's thin-skinned fruits are smaller and darker than the cooler climate Lisbon's fruits. Even in tubs the tree trunks are beginning to thicken. Wet-skinned lemons glow like small suns against grey winter skies. Six potted cumquat trees' cream-splashed and lime-streaked variegated leaves light up darker winter corners. Cumquats hang candy-striped lollypop fruits all year. My friend, neighbour and gardener, Margaret, gave me this recipe for brandied cumquats.

Brandied Cumquats

Place 250 grams of fruit into a preserving jar. Pour a mixture of 250 grams of sugar and 250 mls of brandy over fruit. Refrigerate. Stir every few days until all the sugar is dissolved. Leave for a few weeks before spooning over ice-cream for a no-fuss summer dessert.

From late spring to summer, red poppies poke up through cracks in the stones. Clipped rosemary edging sets off symmetrical hedges of the cream-yellow David Austin rose Windrush.

A massive, rough-hewn table and pair of sun-bleached teak seats furnish the room. Banksia boughs tree-roof shade. In the afternoon a white umbrella is the only cloud in the sky. In summer's meltdown, the pots nag for a drink but splashing water with a hand-held hose and smelling the wet soil is relaxing in the evening cool after a stinking hot day.

At first I bought seconds: cracked, chipped and wonky. Rejects going cheap. I warmed to the tones of terracotta: honey, pumpkin and marmalade, its touchy-feely texture and moss-crusted patina. Scrounged for knock-down prices, from op-shops and junk shops, country car boot and clearing sales, pots piled up. Flower-filled with prissy petunias, corny cactus and you-name-it-I-potted-its. But the pots were itsy-bitsy sizes and grouped any which-way. I considered the BPF factor: Balance, Proportion, Form. I went 'good taste'.

I got diddled on halved oak wine barrels to show-off bay and box. It cost me an arm and a leg for set-of-six terracotta tubs. Mobile gardens were dragged by the rims, rolled or humped onto barrows and strategically 'back a bit' 'more to the left' located around the garden until they were just right. Pots bring the garden home all through the seasons when I pinch off a few basil leaves in summer or brush my hand across lemon thyme scrambling by the back door.

When guests come for a get-together, we rise early. On non-fire-ban days we light the rusty outdoor oven set in the fireplace for a big bake-up. Leaf litter flutters into the fire. Red-glow bracken burns to ash. The furnace is fed with snap-dry twigs, banksia cones and bundles of tea-tree prunings. Smoke scraps whoosh from the flue, billow up and stain the sky. Eucalyptus, fish and garlic smells waft through the bush.

We hang around in the courtyard and dine alfresco. The evening meal is simple. Olive flat bread, crusty pizzas loaded with fetta, tomato and basil, platters of charred capsicum, eggplant, small-catch fish wrapped in oiled vine leaves and grate-grilled crispy fish served with burnt bits and lemon wedges. Dry bay leaves, rosemary and tea-tree crackle in the coals. A mosquito coil spirals smoke.

We unwind, sniffing in rose and lemon blossom perfumes that hang in the air, trapped by the fence, wall and sun-stored stone. Moths dust our shadowed faces. Strings of party lights loop across overhanging banksia branches. Sea hum and laughter echo into the night, washed with waves. Above, the sky is lit with the single star of Venus and a pearly abalone shell moon. The rich smells transport me to an outdoor Greek taverna. If I close my eyes and sniff the lavender, rosemary and citrus scents, the banksias transform to stony olive groves. We spill chianti, spit olive pips, tear bread, top-up our glasses, toast the garden and give summer a send-off.

Sharing yarns, wine, good tucker and fine company in such a setting makes a garden worth the effort.

VISITORS

I always intended the garden would be kept a have-you-to-myself secret. Our gardens are our own private paradise. Going public seems a contradiction.

In my stretch of the imagination, the garden flourished with date palms, persimmons and pomegranates. It was perfumed with camphor, cinnamon and frankincense. I fantasised that it would remain as a medieval monastery, cloistered in Kashmir or Tibet, parterred with herbs and clipped knot hedges. The only sound to break the silence would be the tinkle of a bell for morning meditation.

But reality bites. It was time for it to make its own way in the world. Shattering flights of fancy and wearing my heart on my sleeve, on the dreaded day one November I flung open the gates and took a deep breath.

Friends Chris and Liz assured us, 'You'll be beating them off with a stick.' But would anyone turn up? They didn't. Not at first. (Apart from Chris and Liz who dropped by for a sneak preview before the season opened.) We hadn't made it easy. Parking was restricted to the elderly and disabled. Everyone else was expected to walk the two-hundred-metre track into the out-of-the-way property. We didn't spruik for business. There were no billboard posters to pull the crowds. It wasn't on the 'must-see' or 'worth-a-look' list. It had no street cred. The only advertising was a plug in the local paper and a few pamphlets left at the general store. A handful of scouts braved the first weekend. Hardly a full house or standing room only. But the word got out.

I was struck with panic. I worked alone. The thought of being stampeded by marauding mobs was scary. I bit my nails down to the quick. I stuttered whenever anyone mentioned the words 'Open Garden Scheme'. Pictures need space. Perspective would change. The area would shrink. Self-doubt crept in. I feared a flop.

Garden viewing is voyeurism. It's an up-close-and-personal. It's a Peeping Tom peek-hole into the person who made it. It's a self-portrait, an autobiography of triumphs, stuff-ups and glaring mistakes. Following paths is like tracing the palm lines of the gardener's hand: headline, heartline and lifeline, scabs, scars, warts and all. Exposing your garden to the public eye is like standing in your underwear. If it's not up to scratch you're caught with your pants down.

The garden became a stage set in an open-air theatre, starring plants as performers. Some of the cast-of-thousands proved touchy. Beans were highly strung. Potatoes were thin-skinned. Chillies got hot headed. Liliums played shy, sweet peas sulked and fennel was fickle. Superstars hogged the spotlight. Others played prima donna, refusing to make guest appearances. Wannabies waited in the wings. Has-beens missed their cues. Up-and-comings couldn't get their timing right. Could we pull it off? Somehow it would get its act together, even if it was under-rehearsed.

Sometimes it felt more like a sideshow. Roll up. Roll up. Ladies and gentlemen. See world-famous plants strut their stuff. The death-defying strongman succulent. The bearded lady iris. Cannas swallowing flames. See the human gardener jump through hoops. Step this way. I felt as if I was the stand-up support act: a lady sawn-in-half, juggling selling plants, learning my lines for a speaking part and balancing a queue of visitors all at the same time. Despite wishing, hoping and praying, the weather was always a lucky dip. We copped freak storms. But even on horror days in don't-die-on-me-now 40-degree heat or 70-knot gale-force winds, despite the shambles, 'The show must go on'.

Would we wow them or be laughed off the stage? Would it be a jaw-dropper, eye-popper showstopper? A sell-out? Would there be gasps and gazes-in-wonder? So-so's? Oh no's? Oohs and aahs? Ha ha ha's? Hisses? Boos? Rave reviews? Hardly. Just-scrape-through would have to do.

Behind the scenes the backstage crew got in on the act: clouds on curtain call and sun on low-tech lighting. Wind assisted with sound and special effects. Birds ad-libbed. The sea murmured like an audience.

Preparation was a set-up. Plants were briefed. I lived with the guilt of resorting to last-minute window dressing, gimmicks and cheap tricks. I took short cuts. The garden was dressed up in a hire suit for the occasion. I felt like a stagehand shifting scenery. Stand-in show ponies were stuffed into bare patches. Ready-made punnets tarted up dull beds. In a weak moment I filled gaps with one-day wonders. Off-stage I slipped in and out of various characters. I played the part of director and masquerader of 'tidy-gardener' faking a day-in-the-life-of-a-well-kept garden. I was a fraud. Wind would blow the disguise.

A garden is an ongoing process. It is never 'finished'. The first year we unlocked the gates, ours was downright incomplete. The makeshift fence was propped up with chicken wire. Half-built stone walls appeared abandoned. The yet-to-be-built lichgate entrance was still on the drawing board. The courtyard was in its infancy. The red rose garden was just a twinkle in my eye. I had carried the garden from conception to delivery but its difficult childhood was yet to come. I practised my apologies.

But I was taking it too seriously. I got over it and I stopped playing drama queen. I recovered from pre-public jitters and saw it not as a competition but as a celebration of what we had achieved. In more deluded moments I had tickets on myself. I grandstanded. I felt giddy with pride, a sense of smug satisfaction, and secretly awaited compliments.

My early fears were unfounded. No one nudged elbows, rolled their eyes or mumbled 'not a patch on Sissinghurst'. When one of my old out-on-an-excursion teachers fronted for Show-and-Tell I sat up straight and paid attention. I imagined my report card: 'Good try Paula but could do better'. All-smiles and 'love your work' gave it a big tick and an elephant stamp. Visitors who came back for more each spring watched the garden evolve. They knew their way around. They felt as if they were part of something. 'The tomatoes are going to be early this season.' 'The roses were a bit of a worry last year but are coming along nicely.' They noted its progress. 'Those rosemary hedges have taken off.'

While gardeners loved the ambience of the place they always hit me with the same questions: 'Where are the compost bins?' 'What do you do for water?' 'Where do you get your mulch?'

These set-me-straight questions got tell-it-like-it-is answers. Behind those sheets of scrap iron. Give the petrol pump a yank. The tip. The working vegetable garden always attracted the most attention.

First-time visitors spoke in lowered voices as if stepping on sacred ground. But after a leisurely map-in-hand stroll this all changed. Gardeners buzzed around the urn like bees around a hive. Under the shade of a tea-tree marquee and borrowed beach umbrella, guests felt at home rummaging in cake tins for slabs of hedgehog and dunking melting moments into cups of lukewarm tea. Laughter percolated. Garden lovers loosened up. They got chatty, got the goss and rattled on. Gardens speak a universal language that breaks down social barriers.

Some day-trippers checked out more than a cultivated garden. They took in the wild gardens. Open daily. Free entry. They wandered down to the beach, swam in the surf, rambled in the Reserve and caught the wind-blown beauty of the coastline. Nature is a clever caretaker of its indigenous gardens. It doesn't lift a finger. Wind plants seed. Rain waters. It self-mulches. Maintenance-free, it looks good all year round.

But what was in it for us? Well, we didn't get rich quick. We didn't rake in the bucks. But opening your garden has pay-offs. It's a swift kick up the bum to reach goals and meet deadlines. It lifts your game. You get to rub elbows and shake hands with home gardeners. You meet kindred spirits. You score personal invites to gardens on a you-showed-me-yours now-I'll-show-you-mine basis.

When the weather behaved, some guests spread a rug, slumped back, opened a bottle of wine, picnicked on sandwiches, olives and cheeses, soaked in some sun and had a hoot. Melbourne Cup weekend was the equivalent of our own Spring Garden-Party Racing Carnival. As a trainer I felt jumpy. Track side the crowds dressed for fashions on the field in broad-brimmed raffia, floppy terry-towelling hats and binocular-sunnies, taking a ten to one punt on the weather, a flutter on the annual event or hoping to back a winner.

Shot-silk poppy jackets shimmered in the sunlight. Daffodils jumped the gun. Foxgloves leapt from the starting stalls. Way out in front, sprinting annuals set a cracking pace. Opium poppies rode high in the saddles jockeying for the best position. Cardoons plodded along at the rear. Hollyhocks struggled to keep up, finishing lengths behind despite their long stride. The crowd whooped with joy as champion roses flashed along the home stretch pipping the post for a photo finish.

Viewing gardens feeds the dream. It broadens horizons and opens windows to wider worlds. No matter how many armchair gardens you visit in books, nothing can replace getting out there and experiencing the real thing. Open gardens can send your senses spinning and your head buzzing. They can humble, tease and turn you grass-is-greener green with envy. They can make you want to rush home, trash your own second-rate efforts and begin again.

Ploughing through gardens can sow the seed to harvest new ideas. My visits to John and Sunday Reed's Heide garden opened doors of insight. The charm and vision of Edna Walling's Bickleigh Vale village at Mooroolbark inspired building the cottage. Castlemaine's memorable Buda introduced me to a tree paeony. A Grampians garden was where Madame Hardy's and my green eyes met across a crowded room.

After the crowds did their disappearing act it was always good to reclaim the space, board up the gates and hang the 'Sorry We Are Closed' sign.

Despite truckloads of plant buffs, nothing was knocked off. No one stripped plants bare. There were no trampled beds or walked-on flowers. Some snapped off seed pods and pinched off cuttings but no harm done. Gardeners are generally considerate. Many swapped plants, shared seeds or bartered a bucket of lemons. The garden grew up. Guests felt they were in on a secret. The richest reward of opening the garden has been the friendships formed.

I sometimes wonder, though, how I'd feel if the garden were kept hush hush. If it never made its debut. I think it would be the equivalent of a hand-made suit packed in mothballs and never worn. A song not sung out loud. A scented love letter never read. Something worthwhile not shared.

REFLECTIONS

The how-the-hell-did-we-do-this garden has grown to something beyond my wildest dreams. It has been influenced by my European heritage, but over time, inspiration has come from the surrounds.

Initially we felt awkward stumbling through this landscape. We were stuck in the Australian mind-set. 'Bush' meant towering eucalypts. Instead we found ourselves in deformed scrub where tortured trunks leaned their heads away from ear-bashing winds.

On the surface this scrub could be devalued and dismissed as insignificant. Drab tones, rough bark, twiggy undergrowth, sharp sword grass, dead bracken stubs and thin soil do not fit the mould of beauty.

It has been a slow dawning. The shift has been gradual. Time has untied the blindfolds. It has refocused our eyes to the intimacy and sensuous richness of a wonderland: the forest's understated colour and texture, trunk and branch squiggles, grass-thatched dunes, fleeting flowers, curled bracken hooks and a thornbill's freckled eggshell. Our ears have tuned in to the live music of the sound scape: the crackle of seed cones, wing-beat, wind change, seabird song and a mother calling her joey. We taste the salty air, smell the bush's subtle perfume and listen to the silence. We are learning to divine its hidden laws, moods and fluctuating heartbeat.

We underestimated the dimensions of what we set out to do. Growing your own vegetables, collecting and cutting firewood for heating and cooking takes time. Isolation tested our self-reliance. The wind blew our ideals to bits. The sun did not forgive mistakes.

But we have learned from our mistakes. We have learned valuable lessons. We have realised our strengths and limitations. We have come to grips with nature's terms of gardening here and the forces of the seasons: harsh summers, winter's hard-driven rains and spring and autumn's racy winds. But we will never de-mystify this primitive landscape. We will never grasp its dream time aura or be in on its well-kept secrets: where a chrysalis is spun, where moths leave their skeletons or where snakes hibernate. We will always be in awe of its strange marsupials that belong to a pre-human past.

We didn't define a philosophy. Unconsciously we've formed a partnership with the natural world around us. The bush and the garden are entwined. Our children have grown up to the taste of home-grown tomatoes, to value picking an apple from a tree and to love and respect the unique wildlife and its habitat. Their childhood memories are linked with the garden: skinning their knees, pulling baby carrots from their own plots and riding high on their dad's shoulders to come face to face with a giant sunflower.

In twenty years we have absorbed the landscape and seascape where two worlds meet. Our toes have turned into the earth and have taken root. We bend with the winds that whistle around our ears. Like the paperbarks, we've peeled back layers of dead skin.

We have simplified our lives. Loose threads have knotted together as living links. This is a place where we can lie on the grass with our kangaroos, walk empty beaches, enjoy the luxury of solitude, swim in the surf and feel a sense of wilderness and liberation from the modern world.

We are grateful for the garden's gifts as we move with the rhythms around us: the sea rising and falling, buds breaking open, flowers closing, leaves turning to roots, roots turning to leaves, birds coming and going and the spade and the tide and the seasons turning.

PLANT LIST OF COMMON NAMES

Abutilon sp.   Chinese lantern
Acacia sophorae   Coast wattle
Achillea sp.   Yarrow
Allium ampeloprasum   Russian garlic
Allium fistulosum   Welsh bunching onion
Allocasuarina verticillata   She-oak
Anethum graveolens   Dill
Anthemis tinctoria   E.C. Buxton Dyer's chamomile
Artemisia absinthium
Artemisia abrotanum   Lad's love/southernwood
Artemisia ludoviciana
Asparagus officinalis   Asparagus
Avicennia marina   Mangrove
Banksia integrifolia   Coastal banksia
Berberis thunbergii   Barberry
Borago officinalis   Borage
Buddleia crispa   Himalayan buddleia
Buddleia globosa   Chilean buddleia
Buddleia davidii   Butterfly bush
Bursaria spinosa   Sweet bursaria
Calocephalus brownii   Cushion bush
Centranthus ruber   Valerian
Cheiranthus cheiri   Wallflower

Correa alba   Coast correa
Corylus americana   Hazelnut
Cosmos bipinnatus   Cosmos
Cotula coronopifolia   Water buttons
Cydonia oblonga   Quince
Cynara scolymus   Artichoke
Digitalis purpurea   Foxglove
Disphyma australe   Noon flower
Echium candicans   Pride of Madeira
Eschscholzia californica   Californian poppy
Euphorbia wulfenii
Eucalyptus viminalis   Manna gum
Feijoa sellowiana   Feijoa
Foeniculum vulgare purpureum   Bronze fennel
Ficus carica   Fig
Gahnia filum   Chaffy saw-sedge
Helichrysum italicum   Curry plant
Helichrysum petiolare   Everlasting
Hibbertia fasciculata   Guinea flower
Juniperus chinensis hibernica   Juniper
Kniphofia   Red hot poker
Lathyrus odoratus   Sweet pea
Lavandula dentata   French lavender
Lavandula officinalis   English lavender
Leptospermum laevigatum   Tea-tree
Leucopogon parviflorus   Beard heath
Ligustrum ovalifolium aureum   Variegated privet
Lilium longiflorum   Christmas Lily
Lilium regale   Regal lily
Lonicera nitida   Honeysuckle
Lunaria annua   Honesty
Lupinus arboreus   Tree lupin
Lychnis coronaria alba
Marsilea drummondii nardoo
Meconopsis cambrica   Welsh poppy
Melaleuca ericifolia   Paperbark
Myriophyllum aquaticum   Water weed
Narcissus poeticus   Pheasant's eye daffodil
Nepeta x *faassenii*   Catmint
Nepeta   Six Hill's Giant
Nicotiana tabacum   Nightscented tobacco
Nigella damascena   Love-in-the-mist

Olea europaea   Olive
Olearia axillaris   Silver daisy bush
Papaver commutatum   Ladybird
Papaver nudicaule   Iceland poppy
Papaver rhoeas   Corn or Flanders poppy
Papaver somniferum   Opium poppy
Passiflora edulis   Passionfruit
Perilla frutescens   Perilla
Phlomis russeliana   Jerusalem sage
Pittosporum undulatum   Sweet pittosporum
Pyrus pyriformis   Nashi
Romnea coulterii   Tree poppy
Rosmarinus officinalis   Rosemary
Salicornia quinqueflora   Beaded glasswort
Salvia officinalis   Sage
Salvia sclarea var. *turkestanica*   Clary sage
Sambucus gaudichaudiana   Native elderberry
Samolus repens   Creeping brookweed
Santolina chamaecyparissus   Lavender cotton
Scirpus nodosus   Knobby club rush
Senecio lautus   Groundsel
Silene maritima   Sea campion
Sisyrinchium striatum
Solanum aviculare   Kangaroo apple
Spinifex hirsutus   Hairy spinifex
Stachys byzantina   Lamb's ear
Tetragonia tetragonioides   New Zealand or bower spinach
Thymus pseudo-lanuginosus   Woolly thyme
Westringia fruticosa   Coastal rosemary
Wisteria floribunda alba   Wisteria white

BIBLIOGRAPHY

Stephanie Alexander *The Cook's Companion* Viking 1996

Peter Cuffley *Cottage Gardens in Australia* Five Mile Press 1986

Margery Fish *We Made a Garden* Sagapress Inc/Timber Press 1995

Jean Galbraith *Garden In A Valley* Five Mile Press 1885

Gertrude Jekyll *Color Schemes for the Flower Garden* Penguin 1983

Christopher Lloyd *Gardener Cook* Penguin 1997

Graham Pizzey *A Field Guide to the Birds of Australia* Collins 1980

Jane Taylor *The Dry Garden* Lothian 1993

J.H.Willis *Field Guide to the Flowers and Plants of Victoria* Reed 1975

BOOKLETS

Beach and Bush Day Trips South Gippsland Conservation Society 1985

Anderson's Inlet Waders and Waterbirds A. Chapman P. Dann D. Legg South Gippsland Conservation Society 1987

JOURNALS

Journal of the Lady Nelson 1801 Latrobe Library Melbourne